M000164127

WHY THE
TITANIC
SANK

ABOUT THE AUTHOR

W. B. Bartlett is the author of eleven history books including *Titanic: 9 Hours To Hell, The Survivors' Story* ('Quite the best and most level-headed telling of the whole story I have ever read' *The Independent On Sunday*; 'So enthralling that you can almost hear the ghosts of the drowned, pressing to share their memories of that night of terror' *The Daily Mail*), *The Dam Busters: In the Words of the Bomber Crews*, *Legends Of Blood: The Vampire In History & Myth* and *Assassins: The Story Of Medieval Islam's Secret Sect*. He lives in Bournemouth.

WHY THE
TITANIC
SANK

W. B. BARTLETT

AMBERLEY

*To over 1,500 people whose lives were needlessly
lost on 14/15 April 1912*

ACKNOWLEDGMENTS

To Jonathan and all at Amberley who have helped
with this book my sincere thanks, as well as to
family and friends who have helped me on my
Titanic journey

First published 2012

Amberley Publishing
The Hill, Stroud
Gloucestershire, GL5 4EP

www.amberley-books.com

Copyright © W. B. Bartlett, 2012

The right of W. B. Bartlett to be identified as the Author
of this work has been asserted in accordance with the
Copyrights, Designs and Patents Act 1988.

All rights reserved. No part of this book may be reprinted
or reproduced or utilised in any form or by any electronic,
mechanical or other means, now known or hereafter invented,
including photocopying and recording, or in any information
storage or retrieval system, without the permission in writing
from the Publishers.

British Library Cataloguing in Publication Data.
A catalogue record for this book is available from the British Library.

ISBN 978-1-4456-0630-9

Typesetting and Origination by Amberley Publishing.
Printed in Great Britain.

CONTENTS

INTRODUCTION

The news of the accident that had befallen the *Titanic* sent a chill down the spine of many when the first confused headlines were shouted out by newspaper vendors on either side of the Atlantic. The unbelievable tidings resounded around the streets of Southampton and New York and in many other cities too. At first, they suggested that the great liner had been in a collision with an iceberg but was being towed to the nearest port and all aboard her were safe. Only slowly did the truth come out, in stages, as if being grudgingly squeezed out of those who dared not face it.

Only gradually did it become clear that over 1,500 people had died. Southampton was the hardest hit; nearly 600 of the dead were residents of the city. Belfast too would be overwhelmed by the disaster; there were fewer casualties from the city but the shipyards of Harland & Wolff had been responsible for building the ship and the guarantee party sent out to ensure that everything was shipshape about the *Titanic* had gone down to a man.

The homes of the great and the good were affected on both sides of the Atlantic; some of America's leading businessmen had been on the ship and a number of wealthy and famous individuals had died with her or enjoyed fortunate escapes. Less remarked upon was the terrible price paid by some of the third-class passengers on the ship, mostly immigrants setting out with hopes of a better life, only to end their hard years of toil on a freezing cold night in the North Atlantic. Many an Irish village would be sent into mourning by the death of kinfolk who were, in some cases, already effectively lost to them given their relatives' departure for a brave new world which turned out to be a nightmare mirage. It was a scene repeated in other countries – in England of course, but also in Sweden, in other parts of Scandinavia and across the continent of Europe and beyond (there were, for example, over seventy passengers from Lebanon aboard). In some cases, entire families were wiped out.

Flags flew at half-mast in a number of countries and the leaders of some of the most powerful nations in the world offered their condolences with words that betokened their sense of shock and disbelief. Even artists were prompted to turn their craft to memorialising the terrible tragedy. Thomas Hardy was afterwards inspired to pen a short poem, 'The Convergence of the Twain', which, although its language may now appear somewhat antique, delivered some comments that, even allowing for poetic licence, made some very valid points (though some literary critics feel that the words were concerned as much with his doomed relationship with his wife as with the loss of a great ship – Emma Gifford died in 1912 and Hardy's poem was not published until 1915).

Hardy spoke of how 'Jewels in joy designed / To ravish the sensuous mind / Lie lightless, all their sparkles bleared and black and blind'. The ship lay buried 'in a solitude of the sea deep from human vanity', the same vanity that some declared was responsible for *Titanic*'s death. Some wondered why so much attention had been paid to luxury items like swimming pools, squash courts and a gymnasium whilst no one seemed to have bothered very much about more mundane matters such as lifeboats.

Others saw the hand of destiny – or even God – in the disaster. It was as if the ship was fated to sink, and to take to the bottom with her hundreds of passengers and crew. However, these were examples of melodramatic sentimentalising of the event (and there was certainly plenty of melodrama evident in the aftermath). But in reality there was nothing predestined about her fate. This was an altogether avoidable disaster. There were a number of opportunities to avoid the collision, and even after she had struck the iceberg there were missed chances to save hundreds of lives.

This book analyses the reasons why this did not happen. It is too glib to say that the *Titanic* sank because she struck an iceberg. She did not need to hit the berg in the first place. Even when she did, if the collision had happened differently, then the damage might well not have been fatal. In addition, the shortage of lifeboats is well known but does not tell the whole story. Other factors were at work on that fateful night to add to the problem of the shortage and virtually guarantee that boats for all on board would not have resulted in all lives being saved. If things had only been done differently, then the *Titanic* need not have sunk and, even if she did, given the clement conditions, virtually everyone could have been saved. There were many lessons to be learned from this catastrophe.

Specialists affirm that most if not all accidents are caused by a chain reaction of events. One thing after another has to go wrong before disaster ensues. The *Titanic* catastrophe is no exception. There were several key moments when, if a different action had been taken, disaster could have been averted. Some of these moments, involving the design of the ship, took place several years before the finished vessel ever sat in the water. The *Titanic* still serves as an object lesson in the dangers that present themselves when man has too much faith in his inventiveness and ingenuity. As long as human error exists, then any vessel is vulnerable. To quote a cliché, pride comes before a fall.

There should of course be back-up systems in place, in case things do go wrong. But what if man feels such things are superfluous? Hubris has a lot to answer for in the *Titanic* disaster and, if it had not been present, then many lives would not have ended prematurely. In the final analysis, it comes down as much to attitude as to engineering. That is a lesson that should never be forgotten. It was learnt painfully at the time and many important improvements were made as a direct result of the tragedy. However, the passing of time anaesthetises memory whilst lessons, once hard learned, are forgotten. They need to be relearned anew: as the early nineteenth-century German philosopher Hegel said, 'The only thing we learn from history is that we learn nothing from history.' More modern times have seen their own

*Titanic*s – the loss of life from the ultimate shipwreck has been exceeded considerably on several occasions since; the ships involved are just not as famous.

None of these subsequent tragedies has seized hold of the imagination in the way that the *Titanic*'s loss has. This is both a good and a bad thing. A romanticism has built up around the ship which perpetuates her memory and means that the story lives on. But it is a distorted and sentimentalised survival which has obscured the underlying harsh realities around the ship's loss. In the process there is a danger that the real lessons have been forgotten and need to be reflected on for a new generation.

There is in fact a great deal of surviving evidence about what did happen. Much of it comes from two enquiries held after the event. The first of them, held in the USA (first in New York, then in Washington) was chaired by Senator William Alden Smith. The second, held in London shortly after, was presided over by Lord Mersey. Both were flawed investigations. The London enquiry appeared to be the more organised but it failed to ask the right questions of the right people, largely because on some key points it had already made up its mind before hearing evidence.

The American enquiry was much criticised for the fact that it was chaired by someone who obviously knew very little about nautical matters. There was a great deal of debate, often on nationalist lines, about the relative merits of both enquiries, with stinging remarks directed from the British towards the amateurishness of the American inquest and accusations of 'old fogeyism' being hurled back against the British in reply. Yet it is hard not to agree with the sentiments of Alfred Stead, son of one of the lost passengers of the *Titanic*, who said of the 'landlubber' Senator Smith, 'I do not care if he is a Red Indian. His ignorance, if it exists, is excusable ignorance whereas the ignorance of officers and seamen in their duties is criminal negligence.'

What follows attempts to take the reader on a voyage of discovery, to stop and wonder just why the ship went down and why so many people died with her. Over time, many myths have become attached to the *Titanic* story like barnacles to the bottom of a ship. The account that follows strips these away and tells the true story of why the *Titanic* perished. In the process the true lessons of the disaster may be rediscovered. Nothing could be more apposite in terms of remembering the 1,500 people whose lives were cut tragically and needlessly short on 15 April 1912.

I

NATURE SETS ITS TRAP

It was a cold morning on the North Atlantic. After a calm night, the sea had turned slightly choppy. The air temperature remained as it had done since the previous evening, perishing cold, the kind of coldness that sucked the life out of anyone not wrapped up against it. What was most noticeable though was the view: mile after mile of ice, stretching into the distance. And, most memorable of all, like giant fairy-tale castles made of crystal glass, were the floating chunks of broken-off glacier, bergs dozens of feet high dotted along the horizon.

It was a sight of rare beauty and also one of wonder. It was the kind of sight that many people never see – or at most once in a lifetime, if they are lucky. But for those on the spot this was no dream come true; it was the opposite, a nightmare of untellable proportions. Twelve hours before, those there had been surrounded by luxury and opulence on what was deemed one of the safest ships ever built. Now they were marooned on the open sea in twenty lifeboats, some of which were barely afloat, hoping against hope that someone would respond to the wireless messages for help that had been sent out the night before. Whereas on that previous night they had been dressed in their best, now they were a hotchpotch, some still in their best, some in their nightwear, most if not all of them chilled to the bone and nearly all of them wrapped up poorly against the cold. For these people, the icebergs were no things of beauty or wonder, though even in this situation they could have an ambience of majestic grandeur; they were instead harbingers of death.

Just how this change had come about was a remarkable story. There is one element that is responsible for virtually every shipwreck in modern times: human error. Even when an act of war results in the sinking of a vessel, a contributory factor to the wreck – and certainly the number of lives lost as a result of it – is the unpredictable human element. In peacetime it is very rare that a vessel will sink without at least some contribution from human error being involved in the loss. In modern times of course we should be safer than ever with the use of devices such as radar and Global Positioning Systems. Yet accidents still happen, far too often.

It is tempting to assume that the *Titanic* was lost partly because of a lack of modern technological aids, but that would be wrong. Although the equipment she had was less sophisticated than that available in the twenty-first century, it was still enough to avoid the catastrophe. That it was not avoided was, above all, due to human error or, more pertinently, a series of such deficiencies arising mostly from misjudgements that were themselves the result of complacency and the lack of an example. For, before the *Titanic* was lost, there were no recent major shipwrecks that could be definitively attributed to ice, though enough suspicious losses of vessels without trace in ice zones to make a prudent captain cautious. Unfortunately, there were all too few such human beings around in 1912.

Nature often lends a helping hand to shipwrecks by setting traps for the unwary seafarer. In 1912 seamen reckoned on having to deal with two major risks in particular. The first of them was stormy weather. Sometimes the sea could assume mountainous proportions. The sheer force of the waves and the wind combined could shake even the biggest ship around like a little puppy in the mouth of a bull mastiff. With vessels thrown up and down and rocked from side to side, it was accepted as inevitable that such an event – an 'Act of God' as it would widely be termed then – would occasionally result in a ship being lost. Tragic though such events were, generally it was accepted that these things happened from time to time and little could be done to deal with the danger.

But this was never perceived to be a threat to the *Titanic*. Her very size appeared to make her impervious to such a possibility. A passenger remarked of her sister the *Olympic* in 1911 that she was 'the only steamer where the chairs are not fastened to the floor, as no wave is big enough to rock it'. She would be able to ride out the biggest swells and survive the most turbulent buffetings of the wind. In the aftermath of the disaster, it was remarked that an unnamed bystander had been heard to say to Mrs Sylvia Caldwell, a passenger on board, that 'God Himself could not sink this ship' as she was preparing to embark. It may be an apocryphal story, and certainly it would have seemed in 1912 that it was a very sacrilegious comment that tempted fate (or, more accurately, the wrath of God), but it summed up well enough the prevailing attitude to this marvel of man's handiwork at the time.

The other big enemy was fog and this was certainly a risk that sea captains were well aware of and took seriously. A ship might lose her way in the mist and find herself smashed against ragged rocks or stranded ashore. The dangers were well known. For example, in 1890 the steamship *Stella* ploughed into the Casquet Rocks off Alderney in thick fog: she sank in eight minutes with the loss of over 100 lives. Her captain was subsequently censured for failing to slow down because of the poor visibility. Two years after the *Titanic* disaster, the *Empress of Ireland* would sink in the St Lawrence River after being rammed by the Norwegian collier *Storstad*; the liner would sink in fourteen minutes with the loss of over 1,000 lives. Once more, there had been heavy fog. Even in more recent times the liner *Andrea Doria* sank after a similar collision in fog; that was in 1956 when radar was well established but this still did not avoid a fatal collision because of the human factor.

If we did not know the details of the story of the *Titanic*, we might assume that heavy seas or fog were the reason for her loss, but that could not be further from the truth. The sea that night was a flat calm and there was barely a breath of wind. Not a ripple disturbed the surface of the ocean. Nor was there much of a hint of fog (though the lookouts would later talk vaguely of a 'haze' appearing just before the collision). Nothing could have appeared more ordinary than the night of 14 April 1912, a dark, starlit evening where nature seemed to be at her most pacific. And that was exactly the problem.

For, superficially, it appeared that this was a perfect night for sailing, with apparently good visibility to aid the ship's lookouts – such as Frederick Fleet and Reginald Lee, who were on watch as midnight approached. All appeared as normal as could possibly be. But what was not normal was the presence of a huge ice field right in the path of the *Titanic* towards which the ship was sailing, blithely unaware as it seemed, at a high speed of 22 knots. Nobody seemed to be cognisant of the size of the threat or that any real danger was present – though, as we shall see, there was plenty of evidence to suggest that it was.

Second Officer Charles Herbert Lightoller, who would survive the sinking in heroic and almost miraculous circumstances, would later say that 'of course we know now the extraordinary combination of circumstances that existed at the time which you would not meet again once in 100 years; that they should all have existed just on that particular night shows of course that everything was against us'. This almost suggested that the disaster was some kind of Greek tragedy, with the melancholy end a cast-iron certainty from the very first line. But it was not. It was a totally avoidable tragedy made to happen by human error and a sense of hubris that led very experienced seafarers into some catastrophic miscalculations. Nor were the seamen the only culprits:

others, including the ship's owners and the British Board of Trade, were equally culpable and complacent. This was an act of collective manslaughter.

After the *Titanic* disaster, it was abundantly clear just how dangerous ice was. Before it, however, there were few confirmed incidents where it was responsible for the loss of a major vessel. But there were various clues for those who cared to look closely enough. In 1893, another White Star liner, the *Naronic*, set sail from Liverpool headed for New York. She never arrived there. All her passengers were lost along with the ship. Over the following months several bottle messages were washed ashore. One of them spoke of striking an iceberg in a blinding snowstorm. For some reason these messages were dismissed as hoaxes, though quite why anyone should have played such a trick was not clear. This was despite the fact that the British ship *Hummel*, arriving in New York soon afterwards, told of sailing through heavy ice fields. The *Naronic*'s lifeboats were found, empty, later. They were within 100 miles of the position where the *Titanic* was lost.

Another ship, the *Lady of the Lake*, had sunk in 1833 after striking ice en route from Belfast to Quebec. Over 200 people were lost and only 15 survived. That though was of course a long time before the *Titanic* disaster, but she was 250 miles east of Newfoundland, not too far from the site of the most famous of all shipwrecks, and she was sailing in May, a similar time of year.

From time to time, ships would disappear in regions of the ocean where ice was likely to be present and the vessels were never heard of again. With wireless not yet in existence there could only be speculation as to why they had perished in the absence of any survivors, but ice was in many cases a strong possibility. The US Coast Guard's International Ice Patrol estimate that between 1882 and 1890 fourteen ships were lost to ice and forty seriously damaged; this does not include a large number of smaller whalers and fishing vessels that were also sunk. It follows that the threat from ice, if not as widely publicised as it would later be, was significant even before the *Titanic*.

In any event, it did not take a genius to work out that it would do no ship, not even the largest in the world, any good to collide with an iceberg. And Captain E. J. Smith was certainly well aware of the danger. That was not the problem. The problem was that he did not do enough to avoid it.

On 14 April 1912, two paths converged with catastrophic consequences. One path had a very tangible beginning and its point of origin was very clear. It could be pinpointed to Downshire House, an elegant residence in Mayfair, London. It was a prime spot, a well-proportioned mansion which still exists. It was a much sought-after residence and the owner was clearly a man of means. That man was Lord Pirrie, the chairman of Harland & Wolff, the famous Belfast-based shipbuilder. Over a fateful meal in 1907, he and J. Bruce Ismay – the president and managing director of International Mercantile Marine (IMM), which owned the White Star Line after buying it from Ismay a few years previously – discussed tentative plans for a new class of ocean liner, to be bigger and more luxurious than any ever seen. It would become the *Olympic* class of ships, three beautiful, elegant and stately sisters which would encompass the best of everything that was then available.

The point of origin of the other path was much less clear. It had been millions of years in the making. At some unknown point in the Arctic regions, ice had been forming, layer on layer of snow accreting, solidifying, hardening and forming itself, as if by some invisible hand, into slow-moving glaciers. They grew and grew and continued their lumbering but inexorable advance towards the sea. The winter of 1911/12 had been unseasonably mild and much more ice than usual broke off and dropped into the sea ('calving' as it was known in technical circles).

These huge blocks of ice then floated slowly south, taken by the wind and the current – icy leviathans at the mercy of the waves. They would move at a rate of about 12 miles per day towards warmer climes – millions of years in the forming and weeks in the melting. They would be pulled south by the Labrador Current, past Newfoundland, and then would come into contact with the warmer Gulf Stream and would start to disappear. Their life expectancy would not be long then; they would move into balmier waters and milder air and would dissolve as if they had never been there. But in their short sea lives, as the world was about to be terribly reminded, they could do incalculable damage. Two worlds were about to meet: one the world of nature, of indescribable power and majesty, raw, untamed and untameable; the other the world of man – clever, brilliant, superior man, who could conquer even the elements. The world of the latter would be shaken to the core by what was about to happen.

Nowadays these glacial hazards are monitored carefully as they make their way south. Ships are given every warning possible of the danger that is present and steer well clear of the threat. This is the responsibility of the International Ice Patrol. But the organisation did not exist in 1912, for the *Titanic* had not yet sunk. In the blinding glare of the *Titanic* story, its drama, its pathos and its terror, we can lose sight of just how important the disaster was in a practical sense. Sweeping changes would be made in its aftermath. The formation of the International Ice Patrol was one of them. It would come into being formally in 1914 (though steps would be taken to monitor ice immediately after the loss of the *Titanic* and would remain in place thereafter), specifically because of the disaster, and the organisation still proudly claims, nearly a hundred years later, that no ship that has heeded its warnings has ever collided with an iceberg.

But even before the IIP's formation, it was not that ships were oblivious to the danger. The shipping lanes were moved south every year to take account of the possible threat of ice. Ships had to follow a broadly prescribed route when they sailed east or west across the Atlantic. There would be a slightly different course to be followed when sailing east as opposed to going west (the eastern route following a track further to the south) to minimise the risk of accidental collision between ships journeying in different directions. Having a number of ships on the same course also had an important side-effect. It meant that, with the wonderful new invention of wireless, a ship in trouble should always be within easy calling distance of another that could come to its rescue. It was a brilliant theory but it had two major flaws in the execution. First of all, it assumed that all ships would have a wireless operator on board and, secondly, that all vessels would have 24-hour wireless cover. Neither was in fact the case.

The sea lanes were moved south to take account of ice on 14 January 1912. This was a routine measure adopted every January (they would be moved back north again in August: because of the spherical shape of the earth, it meant a shorter, quicker and cheaper voyage for the ships – the distance was shorter by about 200 miles). This was done as part of an international agreement that dated back to 1898. Unfortunately, the move this year did not take account of the unusual ice conditions. Revealingly, the responsible authorities admitted that 'it had become apparent from numerous reports gathered from the Hydrographic Office that the ice season was an extraordinary one and the office took up the question of shifting the steamer lane with its branch office in New York and with the Navy Department'. And when exactly did it do this? On 16 April 1912 – the day after the *Titanic* sank.

In the event, it was decided that their accompanying recommendation was not radical enough and the shipping lanes would be moved even further south than they originally suggested – all this in the space of days following the unbelievable shipwreck. What before had been a reactionary and plodding bureaucratic regulatory regime had all of a sudden been transformed into a slick, fast-moving mechanism for which nothing was too much trouble. The world had changed indeed. Ironically, even this revised southerly course was not enough, for further reports continued to come in in May 1912 that ice was still being spotted in the vicinity of the revised shipping lanes and they were quickly moved still further south. It should also be noted that this was not the first time such a thing had happened. The shipping lanes had been moved further south than normal several times in previous years, sometimes by as much as 60 miles, so if the ice in 1912 was unusual it was not by any means completely unique.

Ice at sea came in all shapes and sizes. There was field ice, long, flowing carpets of the stuff that could stretch for miles. Then there were bergs, loose, rogue rocks of ice, much more dangerous in some ways as they were more difficult to spot. There were also 'growlers', low-lying blocks of ice that would be particularly difficult to identify at a distance. Fourth Officer Boxhall of the *Titanic* was one of the survivors of the wreck and he told how, on the morning after the disaster as the day broke, he could see ice that stretched for miles, 'as far as the eye could see', along with bergs, although he considered that these were not as large by any means as ones he had seen further north in his previous journeys on 'the Canadian trade'. Captain Lord from a nearby ship, the *Californian*, would describe an ice field that he estimated to be 26 miles long and 1–2 miles wide.

But revealingly Boxhall also said that he had never before seen field ice in the region of the Grand Banks (the area off Newfoundland where the *Titanic* sank) and herein lies a clue as to the mindset of those in command of the great ship. No one expected trouble with ice because it was not normally seen so far south at this time of year. Captain Moore of the *Mount Temple*, a veteran of this particular area, said that 'I have never in all my experience known the ice to be so far south'. Captain Rostron of the *Carpathia*, another important participant in the drama, remarked that 'I never remember seeing ice in April on the track'. Even when specific ice warnings were received it was not enough to shake the *Titanic*'s command structure out of its complacency. Something out of the ordinary was going on in April 1912 but it did not have the appropriate effect on those responsible for the *Titanic*'s safety.

Despite Boxhall's statement about the size of the icebergs, it was clear that there were some quite large ones in the area. Captain Lord described those he saw on 15 April, stating that the most easterly were the largest and that some of these were up to 100 feet high. This is consistent with eyewitness accounts of the berg that was struck by the *Titanic* which describe something that was higher than the top deck level on the ship. These large bergs, it turned out, were almost like outlying sentries to the enormous field of ice that lay behind. Unfortunately, their solitariness would make them even more difficult to see, especially at night.

Of course, the largest proportion of an iceberg by far is underwater and therefore unseen by the human eye. Further, this submarine element will be irregular in shape and will sometimes have shelves of ice branching out below the surface. This means that when a ship brushes past such an object it may appear to have had a 'close shave' and missed it, but this would not take account of any collision that could have taken place below the waterline with a part of the iceberg that is jutting out unseen beneath.

Some companies adopted a very cautious attitude towards ice. Captain Moore had very clear instructions from his employers that he was never to enter field ice, even if it seemed to be insignificant and easy to push through. His normal practice was, on approaching ice at night, to stop and wait for daylight. Then, with the benefit of daytime vision, a suitable course could be steered around it. This was also the approach adopted by Captain Lord of the *Californian* some miles north of the *Titanic* on 14 April (exactly how many miles north would prove a point of bitter contention). Unlike Moore he had never been in ice before, but his method was exactly the same; expecting it because of wireless messages his ship had received, he had put on extra lookouts and, as soon as he saw the field ice, stopped his ship for the night.

Senator William Alden Smith, who chaired the American enquiry into the loss of the *Titanic*, would ask what appeared to be a stupid question, namely, 'Do you know what an iceberg is composed of?' Fifth Officer Lowe, another *Titanic* survivor, responded with the flippant remark 'Ice, I suppose, sir.' It was a clever comment but not actually an accurate one. Scientific research showed that they were also quite likely to carry large rocks that had been picked up as the glacier from which the bergs had formed moved ponderously along before calving into the sea.

Scientific evidence was presented to the American enquiry, confirming that it was quite probable that large chunks of rock were most likely present in any berg in the North Atlantic and were particularly common in those which originated in Greenland. The United

States Geological Survey opined that 'such an ice mass, with embedded rock fragments, would be much more effective in ripping open the plates of a ship's hull than a mass of clear ice', though the same writer also conceded that 'ice in such a mass as the berg which was encountered is, however, probably quite competent to produce disastrous results experienced without calling for the presence of any included mass of rock'.

The probable presence of objects other than ice in an iceberg also leads on to consideration of an altogether more important point: Smith might as well have naively asked, 'What colour is an iceberg?' White is the obvious answer but it would be wrong to think of a berg as some brilliant, almost glowing object, clearly visible in the dark. They would indeed sparkle brightly when the sun shone on them, but in its absence they were an altogether different proposition.

They could often appear much darker than might be thought and were therefore difficult to pick out, especially at night. One of the witnesses called to give evidence to the London enquiry was that intrepid Antarctic explorer Sir Ernest Shackleton. His evidence suggested that 'there are many bergs that appear to be black, due to the construction of the berg itself, and also due to the earthy matter and rocks that are in all bergs'. He also pointed out that bergs could 'tip'; that is to say that as they started to melt they could become unstable and what had once been the large chunk below the surface was now above it and vice-versa. If this happened, then 'after a berg has capsized, if it is not of close construction it is more porous and taking up the water does not reflect light in any way'. Shackleton, although much more experienced in the South as opposed to the North Atlantic, told the enquiry that he had seen ice in the North on four or five occasions and twice it had had a 'dark' characteristic.

So in Shackleton's view, rather than them being easily visible, it could be very hard to spot bergs. Nature had laid a trap for unwary sea captains and the *Titanic* was sailing blithely right into it. All that was needed was to add another ingredient to help camouflage the ice and the trap would be sprung. That ingredient was the visibility on the night in question.

14 April 1912 was an extremely dark night with no moon. If there had have been one, then the iceberg would obviously have been much easier to spot. In Shackleton's view, ordinarily on a clear night a large iceberg should have been spotted from 5 miles off. But he then went on to qualify this statement in a way that was important given the conditions pertaining on that particular night. He said that much would depend on the condition of the sea. If it were even slightly disturbed then the breaking of waves on a berg would be a sure indicator that there was one ahead. He said, 'With a dead calm sea there is no sign at all to give you any indication that there is anything there.' He also stated that he had only experienced such flat calm conditions as those pertaining when the *Titanic* was lost twice in twenty years.

Interestingly, he offered the opinion that he would rather be faced with a large field of ice in a known position than have to divert south to avoid the problem. He reasoned that unless a ship were to move a long way south then there was always a danger of coming across a rogue berg, on its own and much harder to spot. It was also notable that he told the enquiry that on a night such as the one when the *Titanic* sank he would expect to see what was known as 'ice blink', a reflection from the edge of the ice field which would make it very clear where it was. No such phenomenon would be seen with a solitary iceberg. In other words, a berg on its own was much more dangerous than a large field of ice.

There was an interesting contrast between what happened on the *Titanic* and what happened to another ship not too many miles away that night. This was the *Californian*, which would send several ice warnings to the *Titanic*. Under her 35-year-old captain, Stanley Lord, the ship had passed several large icebergs in daylight hours and had dutifully relayed warnings of the fact via wireless to other vessels in the vicinity. Lord, who would become embroiled in huge controversy over the role in the *Californian* and his involvement (or otherwise) in the rescue effort when the *Titanic* struck ice, was, like Captain E. J. Smith of the *Titanic*, well aware that his vessel was headed into a danger zone with much ice around, because for several days he had been receiving wireless messages telling him that this was the case. His reactions, though, were rather different.

The ship's log would later show that the weather conditions experienced by the *Californian* that day were, as it progressed, very light winds and a smooth sea. As he moved closer to the vicinity of the ice, Lord took extra precautions. He doubled his lookout so that, as well as a man in the crow's nest, there was also one in the forecastle of the ship. He also took a very close watch himself from the bridge. These extra precautions were taken at about eight o'clock at night. At about twenty minutes past ten he received a report from a lookout that there was ice ahead. Or so Lord initially said to the London enquiry, but he soon after in his evidence corrected himself and said that he thought that he had personally spotted the ice before his lookouts did.

It was a night, Lord noted later, of very strange visibility; 'deceiving' was his own word for it. Despite the fact that he had been straining ahead trying to spot the massive ice field he knew could not be far off, he was only one and a half miles away from it when he saw it. Two things are noticeable about the approach to the imminent arrival in an ice zone that Lord adopted when compared to that employed by Captain Smith. First of all, Lord took important extra steps to increase the lookout. He was expecting to be into the ice that night and was much more cautious as a result – a contrast to what would happen on the *Titanic*. But there was an important similarity in the two approaches too – neither skipper would slow down because of the threat and both relied on the lookout arrangements to identify the approach of ice in good time. But here too there were crucial differences. The maximum speed of the *Californian* was 11 knots, about half that of the *Titanic*. And she was much smaller too. Both factors taken together meant that she would be able to stop or take evasive action because of ice much more quickly.

This was broadly consistent with the approach that would be taken by most sea captains at the time. It turned out that carrying on at full speed even when there was known to be ice around was very much common practice. Most sea captains interviewed as part of the two post-disaster enquiries would confirm that, given good visibility, they would not take any steps to reduce speed in such circumstances and would rely on the adequacy of the lookout arrangements to spot the danger in good time. This, it would clearly transpire, was not a very prudent approach.

By way of explanation, two further points should be considered. First of all, for liners like the *Titanic* there was quite a tight schedule to follow. She, in common with other vessels performing a similar function at the time, was basically providing a shuttle service across the Atlantic. She was due to arrive in New York on Wednesday 17 April and then return to Southampton on Saturday 20 April. Effectively, in the pre-aircraft days of the time, the *Titanic* and her sister ship, the *Olympic*, were providing a ferry service across the Atlantic, with the *Titanic* regularly leaving Southampton on a Wednesday and sailing back from New York on a Saturday. Although there was a small margin of error, any slippage on this could impact on leaving times and subsequent voyages and it would be a race against time to make up any days that were lost, so as not to throw the entire schedule out. To coin a phrase, time was money. Therefore slowing down was to be avoided if at all possible.

Then there was the problem of complacency. It often takes a major disaster to shake people from this. When people take chances and get away with them, they tend to take the same, or even greater, chances in the future. This was not just a problem in 1912; it continued to be so thereafter. It is human nature to do so. Of course increasingly now countermeasures ('fail-safe' devices) are employed to guard against the human element but sometimes some blindingly obvious dangers can be missed.

Take for example the loss of the ferry the *Herald of Free Enterprise* just outside Zeebrugge harbour in 1987. The ship sailed out of port with its bow loading doors open. Clearly this was undesirable but that was not the first time it had happened. But despite this there was no warning light on the bridge to inform the officer in charge of the vessel of the danger. The crewman who should have shut the doors failed to do so and others who noticed did not consider it their job to take corrective action. As a result of this chain of errors, the ship capsized and nearly 200 people died.

In the enquiry that followed the loss of the *Herald of Free Enterprise*, the concluding report noted that a 'disease of sloppiness' had in fact taken hold of her owners. Yet such ships had sailed for years with no correction to the obviously weak procedures to deal with the problem of open bow doors. The problem was even greater in 1912 as the pressure to race across the Atlantic unless there were obvious problems with visibility continued unabated. In the event, it was not just the shipping companies at fault. There was also a problem with the regulatory body, the Board of Trade, on the subject of speed limits. It would transpire that this was far from the only issue.

At any event, on 14 April 1912, as soon as he saw the ice, Captain Lord on the *Californian* stopped his ship. He had never been in an ice field before and he would not be taking any chances in this unfamiliar environment, fraught with danger as it appeared to be. He could not see the ice field that well in the darkness but he sensed that it was big. Morning light the next day would show him to be right: it was massive. But on the night of 14 April he was just aware of a vague but serious menace looming right ahead of him. So far, Lord had acted in the main in exemplary fashion. For a while he continued to do so. Soon afterwards he sought out the *Californian*'s wireless operator and asked him if he had picked up any ships in the vicinity. The operator, Cyril Evans, said yes, he had – the *Titanic*. Lord instructed him to inform her of the ice that they had stopped for. Evans dutifully set out to do so.

Before this, however, something else had happened on the *Californian*. Shortly after he had stopped, Lord saw a steamer's light approaching from the east (he thought it was about 11 p.m.). Lord recalled that he said specifically to Cyril Evans shortly afterwards when he instructed him to send the ice warning that he was sure the ship he could see what was *not* the *Titanic*. As the other ship had got closer to him – 6 or 7 miles to the south he estimated – he did not see the blaze of light he would expect from the decks of such a massive vessel.

Lord carried on watching the other ship, which he considered 'something like ourselves'. The *Californian* was a medium-sized steamer and of a very different scale and in a very different league from the *Titanic*. He ordered his Third Officer to contact her by Morse light (a device that used flashes of light to send Morse signals), which was done but there was no response. At about half past eleven or shortly after, *Californian* time (ship's time varied depended on how far west or east they were and was updated twice a day – therefore there is no guarantee that this was the same official time as it was on the *Titanic*), Lord could see that the other ship was stopped. He presumed that it was for the same reason that he had – because of the ice.

Lord went down below to catch up on his sleep at about a quarter past midnight. He was confident that, with the ship stopped, there was no real danger and he therefore handed over the bridge to his Second Officer, Herbert Stone, expecting a quiet night.

The fact that he was convinced that the nearby ship was not the *Titanic* might appear to be conclusive evidence that the *Californian* was not that close to the famous liner. However, there was an alternative witness, the *Californian*'s Third Officer, Charles Groves, with a different point of view. He had been on the bridge at about 11.10 p.m. when he saw a ship approaching from the east. He recognised her as a passenger liner, on which he could see a lot of light. Captain Lord was off the bridge at the time – he said that he saw the approaching light from 'on deck' so presumably was watching the same ship but from a different spot – but had left instructions that he was to be informed if Groves picked up any other ships in the area.

Groves duly informed the captain of his sighting and Lord later returned to the bridge. There then followed, according to Groves, a difference of opinion, with Lord believing the ship they could see was not a passenger steamer and Groves convinced that she was. He told the captain that as she stopped, she put her lights out. At any event, Groves agreed that he did indeed try to contact the other vessel with a Morse light. At one stage he thought he might have had an answer but he could not be sure. Certainly no effective communication was entered into with the other ship.

By the time that Lord had returned to the bridge, the other ship had definitely stopped for the night. To reiterate, the captain and his Third Officer differed in their evidence over the type of the ship they could see, with the latter convinced he had seen a passenger liner with a lot of lights. Groves told Lord at the time that the ship he could see had stopped at 11.40 p.m., *Californian* time. At 11.40 p.m. *Titanic* time, the world's largest ship had had a fatal encounter with an iceberg. The debate would later begin in earnest: was this a coincidence or was the *Californian* witnessing *Titanic*'s catastrophic night beginning to unfold?

2

THE ICE WARNINGS

The first precondition for disaster was in place: a massive ice field that was very unusual in the vicinity for the time of year. Nature would compound the difficulty by making the night of 14 April one of unhelpful conditions in other ways. The absence of a full moon would make it very dark on that particular night and the lack of any waves breaking on icebergs would make danger difficult to spot. This made conditions potentially very dangerous indeed. However, this did not cause the disaster – it only created the conditions for it. For catastrophe to ensue, those in command on board the *Titanic* would have to act in a certain manner and sail heedlessly into the trap. At any stage, even minutes before the ice was struck, one different action on the part of Captain Smith and his senior officers would have averted the tragedy. Then *Titanic* would now just be a minor and long-forgotten footnote in history.

It was about twenty to ten on the night of Sunday 14 April 1912. The *Titanic* was starting to close down for the night; back then the Sabbath day was treated with a semblance of traditional respect as a day of rest. There were a few dinners still being consumed but the most noise perhaps emanated from the Saloon, where community hymn-singing had started at 8.30 p.m. (though there were a few card schools that, sacrilegiously in the eyes of some strait-laced contemporaries, continued into the night). Otherwise this was a very peaceful night, with most passengers deciding to turn in early, encouraged by the bitterly cold air.

Only one place was still frantically busy: the wireless shack, which had a large backlog of messages to send out. It had been a trying voyage for *Titanic*'s two wireless operators. Jack Phillips was the senior operator and Harold Bride was his assistant. Earlier on in the trip the wireless had broken down and it had taken hours to sort the problem out. Wireless was still new; Phillips (aged 25 – he had celebrated his birthday on the maiden voyage) and Bride (22) were part of a new breed of young men responsible for what was then cutting-edge technology (it is no surprise to find that *Titanic* had some of the finest equipment then available). The very newness of Marconi's equipment meant that fixing problems was largely one of trial and error and wireless operators had to be mechanics too.

Jack Phillips was the man on duty now, unsurprisingly tired given the frantic pace he had been working at for hours. Sending and receiving messages via Morse was in itself a tiring process, either constant hammering on the keys with the tap-tap-tap of sending messages or listening with great care and interpreting the incoming traffic. Harold Bride was asleep in his berth next door and was due to take over from Phillips later on in the night. Phillips continued through the mountain of social messages he needed to send for wealthy passengers, largely oblivious to anything else. Just then the spark flickered and a message came in from the ship *Mesaba*. It was simple but crucial: 'in latitude 42 degrees North 41 degrees, longitude 49 degrees West to longitude 50 degrees, 30 minutes West, saw much heavy pack ice, weather, good, clear'. It was a mundane message but hinted at the greatest possible threat. It told the *Titanic* that there was a great deal of ice in her path.

Just under an hour later the wireless operator of another nearby ship, the *Californian*, also tried to make contact with the *Titanic*. Not far ahead of the great liner, the much smaller *Californian* had stopped for the night. The reason was simple: the ice field stretching for miles in front of her. Her captain, Stanley Lord, had asked wireless operator Evans if he knew of any other ships close by. Evans had heard the stream of traffic from *Titanic* and realised that she was certainly close. Now the wireless operator of the smaller vessel was trying to let his more illustrious neighbour know of the ice problem so that Captain E. J. Smith could take appropriate precautionary action.

The clock moved on another hour and the *Titanic*, moving at high speed, found herself confronted by an iceberg. It was too late to move out of the way. And what had happened to those two messages in the meantime? That from the *Mesaba* lay under a paperweight, undelivered to anyone in authority. It had though at least been received by the *Titanic*. The message begun by Cyril Evans had not even been finished. Jack Phillips, his opposite number on the *Titanic*, had been too busy to take it.

Wireless was still a marvellous new invention in 1912 (it was not in the sense that the twenty-first century would understand the word 'radio', for no verbal messages were relayed, only dots and dashes in Morse code). But no one had really put any structure around how it was used. It did not exist primarily to act as a safety mechanism, even though it had been used in such a fashion to save many lives from the sinking liner *Republic* back in 1909. Rather it was a way for rich passengers to stay in touch with those ashore (when the ship was close enough to send such a message given that the range of wireless was limited).

Jack Phillips was too busy to forward the message from the *Mesaba* to the officer on the bridge because he was catching up with the backlog of trivia he was relaying to the shore. Cyril Evans did not even finish his message because he aroused Phillips's ire when he tried to send it. The *Californian* was relatively close to the *Titanic* and, when Evans began transmission, it almost deafened Phillips. He angrily replied to Evans, 'Keep out! Shut up! You're jamming my signal. I'm working Cape Race.' (This was the nearest shore station on Newfoundland which was the first point of contact for the *Titanic*'s wireless operators as they approached North America.) The social chit-chat that he was forwarding was much more important than any safety message. He had a huge number of messages still to send, he had been working on them without a break for hours, and he was simply too busy to be distracted.

These two events are on their own bad enough, but they were only the last in a string of missed opportunities. A number of communications had been received which collectively told the skipper of the *Titanic* that there was ice ahead and even where it approximately was. One of the things that nearly everyone agreed about in the aftermath of the disaster was that the regulation of the fledgling wireless industry could simply not go on as it was.

There is evidence indeed, though it is rarely referred to, that the *Titanic* was well aware that there was ice ahead even before she set sail. Fourth Officer Boxhall, interviewed as part of the American enquiry that followed the catastrophe, on the subject of ice told his audience that 'the Captain gave me some wireless messages from Southampton, I think, that we had had before we had sailed, and asked me to put these positions on the chart' (he later told the London enquiry that he might have been wrong, and it could have been Queenstown, but that was still days before the ice field was approached).

Then on the evening of 12 April the French ship *La Touraine* contacted *Titanic* to say that she had passed through ice on her way back to Europe. Positions were duly marked up on the chart by Boxhall with the word 'ice' against the spot marked, but it was not made clear if this was just one berg that had been spotted or a substantial ice field. It appears that not a great deal was made of this potentially vital information.

As *Titanic* moved ever closer to her appointment with destiny, more warnings came in. At 9 a.m. on 14 April, one was transmitted from the *Caronia*. This gave very precise and potentially worrying information, reporting ice in the region of 42 degrees North, 49 to 51 degrees West. This suggested ice over a wide area, not just isolated examples of it. The *Caronia*'s operator was thanked for his information and the message was duly passed on. The message was later passed on to Second Officer Lightoller; after the event this was the first ice warning he could remember hearing about.

At about 11.45 a.m. another warning was received from the Dutch liner *Noordam*. The simple phrase 'much ice' in approximately the same position as that recorded by the *Caronia* again gave potential cause for concern. Another was received from the *Baltic* at 1.42 p.m. Captain Smith received this one and passed it on to Bruce Ismay, chairman of the White Star Line and a non-paying passenger on the ship. Ismay casually put it in his pocket and later regaled some passengers, Mrs Ryerson and Mrs Thayer, with tales of the ice ahead.

Revealingly, Ismay would later admit that even he knew the ship would be in the vicinity of ice that night. Smith later asked for the message back so it could be passed on, though it is not clear that it ever was. He would not request its return for another five hours. This in itself told a tale of how seriously such ice warnings were regarded.

The actions of Smith and Ismay were subsequently rightly criticised, though it is likely that this event made little difference to the demise of the *Titanic*. It should have been brought to the attention of all the officers on watch at once, though it is doubtful that it would have affected the actions being taken. However, it spoke volumes for the casualness with which the ice warnings were treated and gives an insight into the state of mind of the senior officers on the *Titanic*. It would also make it look as if Ismay was taking a part in the navigational decisions of the ship – he would have much cause to regret this incident later.

The liner *Amerika* also sent over an ice warning at 11.45 New York time (about two hours behind the time on *Titanic*). It said that 'Amerika passed two large icebergs in 41 degrees 27 minutes North, 50 degrees 8 minutes West on the 14th of April'. A story would later emerge that the steamship *Rappahannock* had passed through the ice and had passed on a warning to *Titanic* when she passed her. However, the evidence for this is contradictory. An article was cabled to the *New York Times* on 26 April 1912 but it quotes the date that the *Rappahannock* passed *Titanic* as the night of 13 April, a whole day before the collision, and mentions nothing about a warning being sent.

What is in much less doubt is that at around half past seven in the evening of 14 April, the wireless operators on *Titanic* overheard a radio conversation between the *Californian* and the *Antillian*. It stated, 'Six-thirty pm, apparent ship's time; latitude 42 degrees 3 minutes North, longitude 40 degrees, 9 minutes West. Three large bergs 5 miles to the southward of us. Regards. Lord.' Harold Bride took the message up to the bridge, though Captain Smith did not receive it directly as he was at dinner.

The message, which had been sent by the long-suffering Cyril Evans, was originally meant for *Titanic* herself, but Bride was too busy catching up with his accounts to answer it. He therefore got it second-hand from the *Antillian*, meaning that there was a delay in receiving the information, though in the event this was not crucial.

But the delay in passing the information on with this latest message hints at one of the two major problems present regarding the ice warnings which were going to provide another link in the chain reaction to disaster. Harold Bride was doing his accounts because the wireless activities on board ship were run as a commercial operation and not as a safety feature. The wireless operators were not even employees of the White Star Line and instead worked for the Marconi Company. Whilst they were on *Titanic* they set their own agenda with little, or usually no, interference from anyone else on the ship, even the captain. It was true that in situations of known danger they were to make safety messages their priority and, after *Titanic* had struck the iceberg, they were quickly contacted by Captain Smith and put into action. But, by then, it was all too late.

The novelty of wireless was still very real and the large backlog of social messages still to pass on was great business – each one of them earned Marconi good money. But in some ways *Titanic* was better off than many of her contemporaries. She at least had two operators to spread the load whilst many others had none – there was no legal requirement for ships to have wireless on board. And those with one operator of course could not expect him to stay awake for days without any sleep. In practice, most wireless operators who single-handedly provided services on their ships chose to close down the equipment at night. From a commercial viewpoint this made sense – most social traffic was submitted during the day. But by definition the night, with the darkness and the unseen threat, is also the most dangerous time for a ship at sea and the moment when a crisis is most likely to arise with an urgent response required. But if there is no wireless operator awake on other ships to receive a distress call then any SOS (or CQD as the standard signal had been – it had just been changed) might go unheeded.

The generally unregulated position of the wireless operators was also worsened because there were several different versions of Morse code in use, making the understanding of messages something of a lottery. To add to the problems, there was intense rivalry between the wireless operators of different shipping lines and this led to some quite cavalier and unprofessional behaviour. Jack Phillips's rude rebuff of Cyril Evans's doomed attempt to warn him of the ice ahead was a very good example. Another came later in the night. There was an exchange of communication between *Titanic* and the German ship *Frankfurt*. The latter had difficulties making out *Titanic*'s position and Phillips soon lost his temper with him. In the end Phillips told the *Frankfurt*'s operator 'you are a fool. Keep out', effectively closing down the conversation. By this time *Titanic* was sinking. As it happened the *Frankfurt* was too far away to help, but no one knew that at the time.

So the attitude of the wireless operators towards ice messages was less than prudent. In the event both Phillips and Bride acted heroically after the iceberg was struck, staying at their posts until the ship was virtually underwater and the power had gone. Their carefree attitude towards the ice warnings was much more representative of commonplace complacency amongst the wireless operators as a group and not their own individual foibles.

In any event they did pass the earlier warnings on in good time with plenty of warning for Captain Smith to take evasive action. He did little, apart from move his course marginally to the south – perhaps some 7 miles more south than normal, not far enough, as it happened. This raises a second question: can we be sure that if the wireless operators had passed on the later warnings from the *Mesaba* and *Californian*, anything would have been done with them? There was already sufficient evidence to warn of danger ahead without these and yet very little had been done to take extra precautions.

When the fateful collision occurred, Captain Smith was resting in his cabin and the ship was effectively under the command of First Officer William Murdoch, who unfortunately did not survive the disaster. On the watch immediately preceding, Second Officer Charles Lightoller was in charge on the bridge. Fourth Officer Boxhall was also present on the bridge and gave evidence to both the British and American enquiries that tried, with limited success, to establish the truth.

Cross-examined in the USA, Boxhall told the listening audience that no one on the bridge had mentioned the looming risk of ice to him. Strangely, Boxhall – who was responsible later for establishing the ship's position and also for plotting ice warnings on the chart – said that 'I did not realise the ship was so near the ice field'. Yet he had been present when Captain Smith had established the ship's position and marked it on the chart at just before 8 p.m. An experienced seafarer should have been able to see easily enough when they were close to the ice.

Boxhall also told the enquiries that he had received no warnings of ice to add to the chart after that received from the *Caronia*. This leaves several specific warnings, some of which at least had been passed on from the wireless operators to Captain Smith, which he had not been told about. As he seems to have been the man that the skipper was charging with keeping the charts up to date, this seems somewhat odd.

Boxhall remembered marking the warning from the *Caronia* on the chart. But he had no recollection of the warning from the *Amerika* being passed on to him for similar action. Neither did he recall the message from the *Baltic*. He was unaware of *California*'s warning early in the evening of 14 April, though he was confident that all the ice he had plotted from the warnings received was to the north of the track that *Titanic* was on.

At the British enquiry, Boxhall was asked to plot all the warnings on a chart once again. It must have been an embarrassing experience, for when all the various warnings were plotted it revealed a vast expanse of ice (though it is true that these included the warnings from the *Mesaba* which definitively never reached the bridge). The tragedy of course was that no one on the bridge appears to have done the same thing on the night of the accident. If they had done so then they would have been fully aware of the danger they were speeding towards. When asked whether he could explain how *Titanic* had managed to get herself embroiled in this ice field in the first place, Boxhall was limply forced to agree, 'No, Sir, I cannot.' Perhaps Second Officer Lightoller offered a clue; he would say that there was a noticeboard put up in the chart room with warnings attached to it – 'It is open to anyone to look at it,' he would suggest as if looking out for ice warnings was an optional extra of an officer's job.

As First Officer Murdoch, who was on the bridge when the iceberg was struck, was lost, the most informed surviving senior officer was Lightoller, who was in charge of the watch immediately before him and gave Murdoch a briefing at 10 p.m. when he was relieved. Lightoller later told the American enquiry that he did not know that they were in the vicinity of icebergs at the time, which again raises the question of 'why not?' when so many warnings had been received (he later anyway appeared to contradict himself in the London enquiry). But he also told the same audience that, even though he did not see the collision, he immediately assumed that *Titanic* had struck ice. He was also very vague as to which ice warnings he had heard about and which he had not but did recall that he briefly apprised Murdoch of one specific warning. There was not much conversation at the time as to its significance, but Lightoller did recall that they agreed they should be in the region of the ice at sometime around 11 p.m.

Murdoch and Lightoller had also talked about an ice warning much earlier in the day at 1 p.m. when the two men swapped shifts at lunchtime. Captain Smith had told Lightoller of the warning received from the *Caronia* about fifteen minutes earlier. Lightoller returned to the bridge for his four-hour shift at 6 p.m. Despite the fact that several more warnings had been received since lunchtime, Lightoller could not recall that Chief Officer

Wilde, from whom he took over, gave him any briefing on them at all.

Lightoller did though relate a very significant conversation with Captain Smith just before 9 p.m. It was a rather general discussion but with some hidden importance. Lightoller said that 'we spoke about the weather; the calmness of the sea; the clearness; about the time we should be getting up towards the vicinity of the ice and how we should recognise it if we should see it – freshening up our minds as to the indications ice gives of its proximity'.

In fact, there was precious little evidence of any 'freshening up of minds' as the ice approached: no diminution of speed, no extra lookouts. Captain Smith was apparently relying on the clearness of the night to spot ice in plenty of time to avoid trouble; he told Lightoller that 'if it was in a slight degree hazy there would be no doubt that we should have to go very slowly'. Smith knew there was ice ahead and was taking a gamble but believed that unless the weather conditions changed any ice would be seen long before it was reached. No doubt as an experienced skipper he had taken many calculated risks before, but on this particular night this would be one throw of the dice too many. Smith went off to his cabin for a rest at 9.20 p.m., his last words to Lightoller being that 'if in the slightest degree doubtful let me know'.

This was rather an extraordinary conversation. They knew there was ice ahead yet they relied on the lookouts spotting it in good time. They knew the bergs would be easier to spot if there were a swell on the sea but they both remarked on how flat the sea was. Anyway, they figured, a berg would be picked up by reflected light. Yet this was a moonless night, so they relied on the reflected light of a star to pick it up. This was not impossible – Captain Rostron of the *Carpathia* would witness such a phenomenon later that evening – but it was nevertheless a gamble, ultimately with people's lives. Strangely too, Sixth Officer Moody had calculated a position and a time that they would be likely to meet the ice. Lightoller felt that it was considerably too far west and therefore too late but he did not contradict him. It was not clear that this made a difference, but it might have done, and it exhibited a rather lax attitude on the bridge.

Nevertheless, aside from this last hint that there was a slighter higher risk of problems than normal, Smith went off to relax for a while with no concerns for the safety of his ship. *Titanic* went on at high speed towards her appointment with the ice in just over two hours' time. Smith disappeared from the scene and would only re-emerge when the situation that his ship was in could not have been more different.

Visibility was clearly the key for the officers. Lightoller told the American enquiry that when he handed over the watch to Murdoch, 'we remarked on the weather, about it being calm, clear. We remarked the distance we could see. We seemed able to see a long distance. Everything was very clear. We could see the stars setting down on the horizon'. He also asserted to the London enquiry that he was confident he would be able to see a 'growler' from a mile and a half off – hopelessly optimistic as it turned out.

Lightoller was later very specific that 'we knew we were in the vicinity of ice', in contradiction to what he had told the American enquiry (but he also said that ships he had been on in previous years had been warned of ice ahead but had subsequently not seen anything, so there may have been an element of complacency on board). But he was also confident that ice would be seen in plenty of time to take evasive action.

Here then was another important step in the chain reaction that led to catastrophe. There were several issues. First of all, the wireless operators had been dilatory in passing on all messages. This reflected current complacent attitudes in the industry. However, this in itself was not the decisive problem, though there is a chance that passing on the later messages might have prompted someone to call Captain Smith to the bridge and he might have ordered precautionary measures to be taken.

Second Officer Lightoller would later state that Jack Phillips, who did not survive the disaster but was alongside him on an upturned collapsible boat for a while before expiring, had told him about the message from the *Mesaba*. Lightoller felt that it was crucial. He stated that 'that delay proved fatal and was the main contributory cause to the loss of that magnificent ship and hundreds of lives. Had I as Officer of the Watch, or the Captain, become aware of the peril lying so close ahead and not instantly slowed down or stopped, we should have been guilty of culpable and criminal negligence.' Yet this was a very different approach to that which had been adopted so far, which was basically to assume that the ice would be seen in plenty of time to take evasive action.

Smith's role was crucial and catastrophic. He had not slowed down so far despite several earlier ice warnings that he knew all about. He had also been slow to pass on information to his senior officers and order all warnings to be plotted on the chart. This would perhaps have prompted a more cautious approach when it became apparent how extensive the ice field was. But even here we cannot be sure that he did not make a 'mental map' of the danger ahead and discount it.

For again this was not the main problem. Captain Smith and several senior officers knew full well that they were in the region of ice. Enough information had been received and assimilated to gauge the danger. In the end, Smith ignored the risk because he was confident of the visibility of the night and the ability of his lookouts to see icebergs in good time. In the final analysis, it was not the non-receipt of wireless messages that led to disaster but a rather hubristic attitude towards the information that they contained. Another link in the chain had been forged.

What part the actions of the wireless operators on the scene played in the loss was considered by the enquiries in both America and London. Question 6 of the London enquiry (a number of questions were laid out in advance for the enquiry to answer) asked, 'what installations for receiving and transmitting messages by wireless telegraphy were on board the "Titanic"' and then went on to consider the number of operators and the general arrangements. As a result of its findings, the enquiry made important recommendations about the number of operators on board, saying that they should be sufficient for a constant service, day or night, on all ships. The enquiry also said that, when ice was reported in future, then ships should either slow down at night or change course to avoid it by a wide margin. Both were very sensible suggestions but, for 1,500 people, far too late.

3

PEERING INTO THE DARKNESS

At 10 p.m. Frederick Fleet and Reginald Lee took their place in the crow's nest. They replaced lookouts Symonds and Jewell, who told them to watch out for small ice, having been briefed to be extra vigilant in a phone call from the bridge to the crow's nest about half an hour before. It was clear that they would be moving into an ice zone very soon. First Officer William Murdoch had taken over from Lightoller and was now effectively in charge of the ship.

As part of the ship's routine, tests of the water that she was sailing through would be made every two hours. Lightoller, who insisted that this was to generally confirm the temperature rather than hint at any proximity of ice, recalled that they showed that it was only 33 or 34 degrees Fahrenheit that night: freezing or barely above. The tests were made by dropping a bucket over the side and then measuring the water temperature when it was drawn back on board. But he insisted that '[the temperature of the] water is absolutely no guide to icebergs'.

Quartermaster Robert Hichens had taken the temperature of the water shortly before 10 p.m. Lightoller had already told him, just after 8 p.m., to go with a message to the carpenter and tell him to take special care of the fresh water as it was likely to freeze during the night. He had overheard the conversation too when Lightoller instructed Sixth Officer Moody to phone up to the lookouts in the crow's nest to take special care to watch out for ice.

Lightoller's views on whether or not the temperature of the water was a warning of ice in the vicinity were at odds with those of Sir Ernest Shackleton, who felt that if there were no wind and the temperature fell abnormally then that might indeed mean that there was ice around. He did, however, concede that the flat calm that night was a very unusual occurrence indeed, a tacit acknowledgement that there were extenuating circumstances. Lightoller's view that a decrease in water temperature was not a sure indicator of ice in the vicinity was supported by Captain Lord of the *Californian*. On the other hand, Captain Moore of the *Mount Temple*, who was vastly experienced in sailing through ice in the North Atlantic and whose ship was to the west of the *Titanic* on 14 April, felt that a drop in water temperature would give no warning of the proximity of a solitary iceberg but could well hint at a large ice field somewhere nearby.

This was of course something of a red herring anyway. The fall in temperature merely added to an impression of something which the *Titanic*'s officers already knew – that they were headed soon into an ice zone. The dropping temperature just reinforced the general impression, indeed the general knowledge, that sometime in the next few hours they would be close to ice.

What was certain was that, as the inky darkness fell, the air temperature got increasingly colder. Few people would be around outside by choice that Sunday night and many would take the chance to enjoy a meal in one of the *Titanic*'s assorted eateries – segregated by which class of ticket a passenger had bought – and then turn in for the night.

Fleet and Lee were due to remain aloft for two hours and twenty minutes. They were on two-hour shifts but the clocks were due to go back at twenty minutes past midnight. This was to take account of the ship's westward movement across time zones and therefore the two lookouts were required to spend an extra twenty minutes in their lofty eerie. It was freezing and this would not have been welcome. All this for £5 per month (about $20 in 1912) plus an extra payment of five shillings to take account of the hardships of being a lookout. It was a mundane but crucial job and few qualifications were required other than a regular eye test. But it also carried a potentially huge responsibility with it.

In the crow's nest there was a telephone by which the lookouts could communicate directly and quickly with the officer in charge on the bridge. There were six lookouts in total and almost miraculously all of them would survive the disaster that was looming. There was also a box which was supposed to hold a set of binoculars. Unfortunately, that night the box was empty.

The lookouts had looked for the binoculars in Southampton but had been told that there weren't any available by Lightoller. This was strange as Fleet had accompanied the *Titanic* from Belfast, where she had been built, over to the south coast of England for her maiden voyage and he had binoculars then. In the space of the few days in between, they had gone astray.

As is so often the case, an apparently innocuous event had led to this. When the *Titanic* had sailed over from Belfast for her maiden voyage from Southampton, her Second Officer – the man responsible for the binoculars – had been David Blair. However, the White Star Line had decided to appoint a different Chief Officer than the one they had originally planned and Chief Officer Henry Wilde had been transferred across from the *Olympic*. It was felt that the experience that he had had of the very similar *Olympic* would help on the new ship.

Unfortunately, this meant a reshuffle on the *Titanic*. She did not need two Chief Officers so the original holder of that important post, William Murdoch, was moved down to First Officer and the original First Officer, Lightoller, to Second. Someone had to miss out and it was David Blair. He took with him the key to the telephone in the crow's nest and, when he left, the binoculars for the lookouts were also mislaid (they may well have been left in the locker in his cabin but Lightoller never came across them). The *Titanic* would also have a change of captain in Southampton; she had been brought successfully from Belfast by Captain Charles Bartlett, who handed her over to Captain E.

J. Smith (though Smith had previously been in charge during *Titanic*'s sea trials and had also been the skipper of the very similar *Olympic*).

Not everyone agreed with the usefulness of binoculars for lookouts. Sir Ernest Shackleton felt that they were not of great use for them and should only be issued to the officer on the bridge. He felt it was easier for a lookout to have his eyes skimming the whole horizon than to have the restricted field of view that would be the case if he were looking through binoculars. They should only ever be used by an officer when something had already been spotted; one could then home in on the object to get more detail.

Second Officer Lightoller was more reserved but stated that the lookouts would not have had them glued to their eyes all the time but would only use them, as Shackleton stated, when an object had been seen with the naked eye, to pick out more detail. Lightoller in fact was in a slightly difficult position. It was the Second Officer's responsibility to issue the binoculars to the lookouts, so in theory the fact that he did not know where they were made him technically culpable. In any event, he could have issued another pair to the lookouts as there were several pairs available for the officers on the bridge and one of them could have gone without so that the lookouts could have a set.

Shackleton's views in particular contrasted somewhat with the opinions of Frederick Fleet, who of course was a dedicated lookout on the ship and had been one for several years before joining the *Titanic*. He insisted later that the binoculars would have enabled the lookouts to spot the fatal iceberg earlier. When asked how much earlier, he replied pointedly, 'enough to get out of the way'.

Another issue with the lookouts were where they were placed. The crow's nest stood about 40 feet above the level of the forecastle (or about 95 feet above the waterline) and the policy on the big White Star ships was to place two men in the semi-circular structure on each watch and to keep the same pairs of men together. On this watch, Fleet took the port side of the crow's nest and Lee the starboard. Together they would continuously scan the horizon ahead looking for possible danger.

But Captain Smith had decided not to place any lookouts at the bow of the ship. However, a number of other captains reckoned that it was easier to see danger from this level than up in the crow's nest. Captain Rostron of the *Carpathia* led a heroic dash through the ice to rescue *Titanic* survivors that night. As soon as he was made aware of the SOS call on the wireless he put in place a number of precautions, realising that he was putting his own ship in danger by speeding into an ice zone. It was his ship's policy to always have a lookout at the front and another in the crow's nest. Faced with greater danger now, he doubled the lookouts at the bow but did not change the number in the crow's nest. Despite the extra precautions, the night was still so dark that his lookouts did not spot ice on the scene of the sinking when they arrived there until it was only a quarter of a mile off.

Rostron would add some further interesting and very pertinent information. A number of other icebergs had been seen prior to arriving at the site of the disaster. On every occasion the officers on the bridge had spotted the bergs before the lookouts had. Rostron reckoned that this was because the officers had more experience of spotting ice at night, were more on their guard for it than the lookouts, and also (and this sounds terribly politically incorrect in a twenty-first-century context) were more 'intelligent'.

When daylight came, Rostron could see, in the vicinity of where the *Titanic* had gone down, twenty-five icebergs between 150 and 200 feet high. There were so many smaller ones that there was no point even trying to count them all. When he looked back, he was shocked by what he saw – many large icebergs behind him that he had passed in the night, any one of which could have done to the *Carpathia* the same as one of them had done to the *Titanic*. Despite the meticulous precautions he had taken, in the dark he had not even been aware that they were there as he charged past them. This provided shocking confirmatory evidence that Captain Smith could have posted a small army of lookouts and they would probably still not have seen the berg that sank the ship until it was too late. The only effective precautions he could have taken were to slow down or change course.

Sir Ernest Shackleton was asked what he would do as regards his lookouts in the region of ice. He felt that it was easier for a man to spot the danger if he were close to the waterline rather than in the crow's nest. His view was that it was 'undoubtedly' advisable to post an extra lookout in the stem of the ship if in an ice zone. In fact, he felt that the man should be taken out of the two that were normally posted in the crow's nest for there was a danger that the two men together were in danger of being distracted by talking to each other whereas one man on his own would devote all his attention to looking ahead for potential danger.

Another crucial factor was that of speed. Here Shackleton's evidence would be at variance with that of most of the captains from the liners of the day. Despite the disaster that would befall him in 1915 when his ship *Endurance* was caught in thick Antarctic ice and slowly crushed to a pulp (though he and all his men survived in an epic journey of survival in seemingly impossible conditions), he was extremely prudent when faced with any ice in his path. He would invariably, he said, slow down in such circumstances.

The *Titanic* had been speeding at nearly 22 knots when she hit. Shackleton was asked what he would have done if sailing at such a speed in the region of ice. He pointedly replied that 'you have no right to go at that speed in an ice zone'. He stated that even when sailing in a ship whose top speed was 6 knots, he would still slow it down for ice.

When Fleet and Lee took up position at 10 p.m. it was a clear, starlit night. Fleet, however, later said that as the shift moved on a slight haze appeared on the horizon. Lee recalled that Fleet had said to him that 'if we can see through that, we will be lucky'. However, Fleet denied that he ever said any such thing. In his view the haze was not much to talk of and did not make a significant difference for the lookouts' ability to see what was ahead of them. Lord Mersey, the chairman of the London enquiry and a man who did not suffer fools (or those he regarded as such) gladly, was blunt in his rejection of Lee's evidence, saying that 'my impression is this, that the man [Lee] was trying to make an excuse for not seeing the iceberg and he thought he could make it out by creating a thick haze'.

It was an uneventful shift. There was little around to see – no sign of any other ships even. But just then, through the thick darkness ahead of Fleet, something ominous materialised. It was a 'black mass' looming far above the waterline. At once, Fleet struck three bells on the warning mechanism that was linked to the officers on duty on the bridge. He then picked up the telephone to talk to them. It was a very simple conversation, laconic even, as if nothing of any great significance was happening. But it was in fact a death warrant.

Fleet enquired 'Are you there?' to which a simple 'Yes' came in response, followed by 'What do you see?' Fleet replied 'Iceberg, right ahead', to which a simple 'Thank you' came back from Sixth Officer Moody in acknowledgement. And that was it. Fleet dropped the phone in his nervousness and then peered ahead once more, more intently this time, wishing that the ship might change course. His mate, Lee, could not take his eyes off the object getting ever larger directly ahead whilst Fleet had been on the phone.

The next few seconds – there were perhaps just forty of them between Fleet sighting the iceberg and the collision – seemed to drag on for an eternity. The 'black mass', small at first, was growing into something huge as it got closer to the ship. But then Fleet could see the *Titanic* moving slowly, oh so slowly, to port. However, it was too late to avoid the berg completely and the starboard side of the ship brushed against the berg, which stood perhaps 75 feet above the water. There was a shower of ice down on to the deck of the *Titanic* as she passed. Fleet noted a slight jarring sensation and a faint grinding noise but nothing more substantial than that.

The iceberg slipped behind the *Titanic* into the darkness. Fleet thought it was a close shave. In reality it was anything but.

This would perhaps be a good time to review the evidence so far. It was clearly the case that there was an exceptional amount of ice in the path of the *Titanic* on that fateful April night. That spelt danger. The weather and visibility conditions accentuated that danger. But there was ample warning from the wireless messages to take corrective action.

No extra lookout precautions had been taken, nor had the lookouts been issued with binoculars. If either situation had been addressed then the deadly berg might have been seen earlier. However, we cannot be sure that this would have been the case. Captain Rostron, despite his very prudent precautions and alertness, had failed to spot massive icebergs in the night. Nor did everyone agree that the binoculars would have made an important difference – though some of the lookouts did, this could in fairness be interpreted as an attempt to excuse their own failure to spot the iceberg in time.

But accusations that the lookouts were not on the ball are unfair. There is no evidence at all to suggest that Fleet and Lee were anything other than conscientious lookouts, peering intently into the darkness to spot any danger. They were a long way into their shift and perhaps boredom had set in, but the biting cold would help to keep them alert. They were also experienced men and, in contrast to the practice on other shipping lines (which rotated ordinary seamen in turns as lookouts), were employed specifically in their role.

Given Rostron's own inability to spot icebergs on such a dark night, there is little reason to suppose that in any circumstances the lookouts could have seen the berg much, if at all, earlier, even if armed with binoculars. Which raises a question – why did the *Titanic* hit a berg whilst the *Carpathia*, travelling at her maximum speed, did not? Luck may of course have played a part, as did the sense of alertness on board the latter ship which does not seem to have been particularly the case on the former.

But there were two other differences which were crucial. The first of them was speed; the *Titanic*, even though not at her theoretical maximum, was travelling some 50 per cent quicker than the *Carpathia*. The second and connected point is size – the *Titanic* after all was the biggest ship afloat. The connection is crucial; a fast-travelling ship with a massive bulk means a phenomenal amount of momentum which must impact on her stopping distance. These factors were to play a crucial part in the fatal collision, along with the steps that were taken to avoid the iceberg as soon as the deadly object had been spotted, and to these key points we will now turn.

4

ALL A QUESTION OF SPEED

This would be a good time to dispose of a myth. After the disaster a story would gain currency that the *Titanic* was after a speed record in her crossing of the Atlantic. It was indeed a prestigious feat to achieve if she had done so and would earn her the coveted 'Blue Riband' if she managed to do it – no money (at least not directly though it might boost sales indirectly) but ample prestige would accrue. That would be very welcome. The transatlantic shipping business was a cut-throat one, with many competitors struggling to compete for customers to ferry across. The price of a ticket, especially for third-class passengers, had dropped dramatically in recent decades and this led to what would now be called a 'volume-driven business', small margins on each customer adding up to big profits when thousands of customers were involved.

This of course was not the only market that *Titanic* was competing in. At the other end of the scale were the rich and famous for whom the crossing offered not only a passage from one side of the Atlantic to the other but also a chance to outshine their rivals on the social scene. Amongst her passengers were J. J. Astor, one of the richest men in the world; Archie Butt, a close adviser to President Taft of the USA; and Dorothy Gibson, a Hollywood movie star. This was the luxury end of the market – a small number of people relatively speaking but big margins to be gained on each of them. (The *Titanic* was also shipping a large amount of mail too, which would also bring in good money.)

There were many competitors to the White Star Line, a number of them British but many from other nations too – the Germans were an especially big rival. But one of the main competitors was another British company, Cunard. The flagships of her fleet were two greyhounds, *Mauretania* and *Lusitania*. They were much smaller than *Titanic* in terms of gross tonnage (though still large enough at around 32,000 tons each) but also several knots quicker. They had been built for speed, whereas the *Olympic*-class ships were aiming for something quite different: style and size. White Star had never in recent times tried to compete on speed. For *Titanic*, breaking the speed record for crossing the Atlantic was a physical impossibility – she was simply not engineered to do so. This, however, had not stopped some of the press suggesting that the *Olympic* when she set out on her maiden voyage was also after such a record.

On the other hand, this should not mislead anyone. By the standards of the time, the *Titanic* was still a very fast ship indeed. And she was going at the fastest speed she ever went when she hurtled into the edge of a known ice field. It does not speak well for risk management policies on board that night.

It would certainly be true to say that the *Titanic* had been playing catch-up in terms of her schedule from the start. Several unfortunate accidents of greater or lesser significance had befallen her elder sister, *Olympic*. This meant that she had been forced to return to Belfast for repair – there was simply no other dock in Britain capable of coping with these leviathans – which meant that work on *Titanic* had stopped whilst she was fixed.

This had delayed *Titanic*'s initial sailing date. Then, on departure day itself, there was another unfortunate hold-up. As *Titanic* was just leaving Southampton docks she passed by the much smaller American liner *New York*. The latter ship was stationary, tied up with substantial hawsers – there had been a coal strike in Britain which meant that most ships were going nowhere; *Titanic*'s maiden voyage was only possible because White Star had drawn on stocks from elsewhere. Suddenly, there was a loud snapping noise. The hawsers broke as if they were made of flimsy cotton and the helpless *New York* was dragged into the slipstream of the *Titanic*. Only prompt and brave action by those on the tugs attending *Titanic*, as well as those on the bridge of the superliner, avoided an accident. But of course this delayed departure.

The *Titanic* then sailed over to Cherbourg and, from there, to Queenstown (now Cobh) in Ireland. At both ports she picked up more passengers, as well as dropping off a few fortunate ones. Then it was off into the vast expanses of the North Atlantic and her appointment with destiny.

The White Star Line always took time to run their ships in when they were new. This was reflected in the miles that *Titanic* did each day on her maiden voyage. On the first day of full steaming (between midday on 11 April and the same time on the 12th) 386 miles were travelled. During the next 24 hours, Friday–Saturday, 519 miles were eaten up, and on Saturday–Sunday 546 miles.

The second day's mileage had been less than expected and the purser told passenger Lawrence Beesley that they would now probably arrive in New York on Wednesday morning rather than Tuesday night as had apparently been expected at one stage. However, such information was later explicitly denied by Bruce Ismay at the American enquiry, where he said that they did aim not to arrive at the lightship off New York until five o'clock Wednesday morning. This, Ismay said, had always been the plan since before leaving Queenstown. As he said, 'there was nothing to be gained by arriving at New York any earlier than that'. After all, arriving too early would miss the chance of making headlines and having large numbers of press photographers on hand to snap the ship's arrival. It would also play havoc with his passengers' onward travel arrangements or hotel bookings in New York.

In fact it was ironic that Ismay was tarred with this particular brush as he was on record as being very opposed to a Tuesday night arrival in New York. He had already been under pressure to get the *Olympic* to adopt a Tuesday night arrival slot but had been persistent in his resistance. Although it would give more time for the ship to be turned around for a return voyage, Ismay noted in a strong reply to Philip Franklin, IMM's vice-president:

> I feel that passengers would be more satisfied to know, when they left here, that they would not land until Wednesday morning, rather than be in a state of uncertainty in regard to this for the whole of the trip. I do not think you can ever have experienced the miseries of a night landing in New York; had you done so, I think your views might be altered.

If anyone was pushing for a Tuesday night arrival in New York, based on this evidence it was not Ismay.

Ismay's reputation would come under heavy attack in the aftermath of the sinking. He had survived by stepping into one of the last boats to leave. This in the event was probably his major 'crime' and sections of the press vilified him, especially those papers owned by Randolph Hearst in America. One paper, the *New York American*, would christen him 'J. Brute Ismay'. He would also be explicitly condemned by some of the participants of the London enquiry for daring not to go down with the ship.

This led to moral judgments on him which fuelled other rumours about his conduct. It was suggested that he had egged Smith on to increase rather than reduce speed. Some passengers suggested that they had heard him pressurising Smith to do so, whilst there was also talk that he had discussed the possibility of a speed test with Chief Engineer Joseph Bell. But to some, it seemed inherently unlikely that the owner of the ship would pressurise his most experienced and respected captain into increasing speed. Indeed, this was expressly contrary to the rule that the captain had absolute authority over all matters nautical the minute he left port until the moment he arrived at the other end of his journey.

It also did not gel well with the White Star Line's very specific written instructions issued to each captain in their fleet that their paramount responsibility was to their passengers and their ship (after all, one might cynically say, accidents are bad for business and a ship is a very expensive asset to have to replace). On previous occasions when a captain had diverted off track for safety reasons he had had to explain himself afterwards, but there was no evidence of anyone ever being censured for doing so.

A quote from those selfsame instructions was that 'you are to dismiss all ideas of competitive passages with other vessels and to concentrate your attention upon a cautious, prudent and ever watchful method of navigation which shall lose time or suffer any temporary inconvenience rather than incur the slightest risk that can be avoided'. These might sound like platitudes but to back it up with hard cash skippers such as Captain Smith of the *Titanic* received substantial bonuses for each trouble-free year they had. Yet for all that, Ismay – who seemed surprisingly uninformed about some aspects of the pride of the White Star fleet – appeared to have a very good knowledge of the distance that the *Titanic* had travelled on each day of her short and ill-fated voyage and the number of revolutions that her engines were making.

Ismay was the subject of implied criticism from Mrs Emily Ryerson, one of the survivors, whose husband had died in the disaster. She was quoted as saying that

Ismay, 'in his brusque manner', had shown her an ice warning. She asked him if the ship would slow down, to which he replied, 'Oh no, we will put on more boilers and get out of it.' Although Ismay admitted that he had shown the ice warning to some of the passengers, he denied absolutely the conversation about speeding the ship up. But the mud had been thrown and it would prove very resistant to any attempts to wipe it off. From then on, Ismay was on the back foot. It was a situation that he would never truly recover from.

Despite the fine words of the White Star instruction manual, one of the major weaknesses in the shipping industry to be revealed by the *Titanic* disaster was the widespread practice of captains not slowing down in areas where ice was known to be present as long as the visibility was satisfactory. In fact, amongst the last of the 25,622 questions asked in the London enquiry were several on this very point that were put to Gerhard Apfeld of the Belgian Red Star Line. He confirmed that it was common practice not to reduce speed in the region of ice and told the court that 'I believe every captain will give you the same answer; they will not slow down unless it becomes thick or hazy'. In the very last question of all, asked of Captain Arthur Tride of the *Manitou*, this was confirmed to be precisely the case.

It was clear after the *Titanic* disaster that this practice must be discontinued; Lord Mersey's judgement on the matter was that Captain Smith

made a mistake, a very grievous mistake, but one in which, in the face of practice and of past experience, negligence cannot be said to have had any part; and in the absence of negligence it is, in my opinion, impossible to fix Captain Smith with any blame. It is, however, to be hoped that the last has been heard of the practice and that for the future it will be abandoned for what we now know to be more prudent and wiser measures. What was a mistake in the case of the *Titanic* would without doubt be negligence in any similar case in the future.

To avoid any chance of doubt, at the start of the enquiry the court had set out questions to be answered as a form of terms of reference. Question 14 (b), following on from the first part of the question about how quickly the ship was going (answer: 'about 22 knots'), simply asked 'was such speed excessive under the circumstances?' The one word answer the enquiry came up with was 'yes'. The final report of the enquiry recommended that in future situations where ice was in the vicinity then ships should either slow down or shift their course to stay well clear of the danger.

During the latter part of its curtailed journey, the *Titanic* had approached a speed of around 22 knots. Not all the boilers were lit yet and there may well have been several more knots in her. Lightoller later said that White Star ships rarely attained their top speed during the first twelve months of sailing and judged that the *Titanic* could ultimately have reached a speed of 24 knots when fully run in. The speed she was travelling at when the collision occurred was the fastest she had ever been and much too fast to stop in time if she spotted an obstruction only a few hundred yards in front of her.

When Fleet sent down his warning to the bridge, Quartermaster Hichens in the wheelhouse suddenly heard three gongs sound, a signal that there was something dead ahead. Then he heard the phone ring, though he could only hear one side of the conversation that followed (Moody's). Then he heard Moody say to First Officer Murdoch, 'Iceberg, right ahead.'

The response was instantaneous. The order rang out from First Officer Murdoch – 'hard astarboard'. All of a sudden multi-tasking, at the same time he was on the telegraph that was wired up to the engine room. Fourth Officer Boxhall, who was just entering the bridge at this very moment, could see that the indicators said 'full speed astern'. Hichens responded to the order to turn the ship at once (the effect of the instruction should be to swing the head of the ship to port) whilst Moody looked on to make sure he was doing what he had been told to do.

It has recently emerged that Second Officer Lightoller believed that Hichens turned the wheel the wrong way, thinking that the ship should be turned to starboard rather than the wheel being turned in that direction, which would swing the ship to port. This is not an impossible occurrence: steering instructions were different for steamers than they were for sailing ships in 1912. However, this goes against the evidence given to the enquiries after the sinking, though in one of these Hichens admitted that he could not see the berg from his position at the wheel, and was therefore effectively steering the ship 'blind' at the crucial moment.

It was later suggested that the instruction to the engine room to go full speed astern was a mistake. It effectively removed turning power from the ship at the moment when it could least be afforded. Effectively putting the ship in reverse in an attempt to stop her would mean that she would proceed on in the same direction she was going when the order was given and the turning motion would be delayed. Just a few seconds could be crucial; but, in the absence of definitive knowledge of the shape and structure of the berg in front, and in particular the existence and extent of any underwater and hidden shelves on her, we cannot be sure how crucial.

Before leaving Belfast, the *Titanic* had undergone a sea trial. It was not in truth that extensive but it did yield up some useful information. One exercise was a stopping test. The ship was put at full speed, then, after passing a buoy that had been placed in the water, she was put full astern to see how quickly she would stop. At about 20 knots, it was noted that it took about half a mile to come to a halt. To put this into context, it would be helpful to know how far away the fatal iceberg was when spotted.

Unfortunately, neither lookout seemed a particularly good judge of distance. Fleet later refused to hazard a guess, though he might well have been intimidated by the nature of the enquiries that he appeared before in both America and London. He after all had a significant part to play in the events of that night and would rightly have been on his guard against being made a scapegoat. Lee was a bit better but not much so; he thought it might have been half a mile away or less: in the event too near for the *Titanic* to stop in time.

Subsequent tests with the *Titanic*'s sister ship, the *Olympic*, suggested that the distance involved was slightly under 500 yards – just over a quarter of a mile – and that it would take the ship 37 seconds to manoeuvre into a similar position that the *Titanic* was in when she struck the berg from the time that the wheel was put hard astarboard. Allowing for the time that messages were relayed to and from the crow's nest a distance of half a mile off when the berg was spotted seems about right. Allowing for delays in responding to the sighting, this gave far too little time to avoid the collision.

Murdoch's plan was to swing the forward part of the ship to port and then swing round the other way so that the stern of the ship might also move clear in the opposite direction (Boxhall overheard Murdoch telling Captain Smith this after the collision – neither man would survive to give their own version of events). However, it was far too late for that manoeuvre to be successfully accomplished. The front of the ship had barely started to swing to port, by barely two points, before they were on top of the berg, even though the wheel was hard over.

In the event, that two points to port was probably fatal. It presented the side of the ship to the berg, allowing the latter to scratch out damage along a substantial stretch of *Titanic* and permitting water to enter a number of watertight compartments. This was catastrophic. The structure of the ship was such that a headlong collision may well have resulted in one or more of the watertight compartments filling up. However, the bulkheads that were inside the ship would limit the damage to these areas. Some lives would inevitably have been lost in the collision but the ship would not sink. She would sag at the bows and look and be very unwieldy in the water. But she would float. However, the slight movement to port exposed a long extent of the ship's side to the danger.

This led to some suggesting that Murdoch's actions were wrong. Bruce Ismay at the American enquiry said that 'if this ship had hit the iceberg head on, in all probability she would be here today'. There was a clear implied criticism of Murdoch's actions here in that Ismay was half-hinting that the First Officer should not have altered course when the berg was spotted as it was too late to get out of the way of it. However, this is being wise after the event. When the berg was spotted, it was the natural reaction to try and avoid it.

The timing of the sighting of the berg was crucial. Just a short time earlier and the *Titanic* might have been able to move out of the way. A short time afterwards would have been too late to start to change direction and the damage would have been limited to the front compartments. Perhaps if luck played any part in the loss, it was more than anything else because of this fatal coincidence of timing.

This new breed of monster ships had experienced several problems already which hinted at the difficulty of manoeuvring them. The near miss with the *New York* in Southampton was one such example. The *Olympic* too had had an accident and a near miss. When docking at the end of her first voyage in New York, the immense suction that the vast bulk of the ship created almost drew in a tug under her stern. An accident was only averted with difficulty.

More seriously, in the previous year the *Olympic* was in Southampton Water when a warship, HMS *Hawke*, passed nearby. She tried to turn hard aport but her helm refused to answer to the command and she instead drifted in the opposite direction. As if attracted by a magnet, the *Hawke* was drawn irresistibly into the side of the *Olympic*. It left a significant hole in the side of the liner but she managed to limp back, listing to starboard, to Southampton without any danger of a full-blown catastrophe occurring despite the fact that two watertight compartments were flooded and a third was partially filled with water. The damage to the *Hawke* though was much more substantial with most of the bow stoved in. It looked as if the front of the ship had been punched flat. A subsequent enquiry found the *Olympic* to blame, the most popular theory being that the massive suction caused by the bulky liner had sucked the smaller ship into the side.

It is perhaps significant that Captain Smith of the *Titanic* had never had an incident of note before these events. There was such a quantum leap in size that it is understandable if these ships were much harder to manoeuvre. Mere statistics can only hint at the problem but, for example, one of Smith's previous ships – at the time the effective flagship of the White Star fleet – was the *Oceanic*. Making her first voyage in 1899, she was also the largest ship in the world at the time. She weighed 17,272 gross tons and was 704 feet long (incidentally, she was also gloriously fitted out, probably even more luxuriously than the *Titanic*). The *Titanic* in comparison was 882 feet long with a gross tonnage of 46,328 tons. It is perhaps notable that the difference in gross tonnage was much more marked than the difference in length, which could suggest much greater difficulty in manoeuvring the much bulkier *Titanic* than the *Oceanic*.

If it were indeed difficult to manoeuvre these leviathans quickly, then it calls into further doubt the wisdom of travelling at 22 knots in the region of ice. Some experts would suggest other problems after the event. One suggestion was that the rudder was far too small for a ship of *Titanic*'s size, for example much smaller proportionately than those of the major Cunard liners. If this were true (and not every expert concurs) then that too would have a significant impact on the ship's ability to turn quickly.

What is anyway incontrovertible was that the *Titanic* made no effort to slow down until it was too late, even though there was a widespread awareness that they were headed into an ice zone (though given the poor communication that epitomised the issue, not everyone was sure where it was). Deep in the bowels of the ship, Leading Stoker Frederick Barrett was responsible for supervising the loading of coal into the vast furnaces that powered the ship forward. It was certainly not cold down here. Sweat covered the men who were constantly loading the coal into the flames. Many of them wore thin singlets – anything warmer would have been unbearable in the suffocating humidity down in the stokeholds.

Barrett was responsible for No. 6 section, far forward on the ship. He supervised a team of eight firemen and four coal trimmers. When the ship struck, he was stationed on the starboard side of the ship. There was a system of lights in the stokehold that acted as a form of communication for the men down there, cut off as they otherwise were from the rest of the ship, another world far above them – they were a long way below the waterline where they were.

The lighting system was simple enough. There were three coloured lights. White meant full speed ahead, blue meant slow and red meant stop. Suddenly the red light came on – a result of Murdoch's telegraph to the engine room. At once, Barrett shouted out the instruction 'shut all dampers'. The men began to do so at once. But before they could complete the task, there was a 'crash' – George Beauchamp, a fireman further forward, described it as like the roar of thunder. At once, water came pouring in about 2 feet above the floor level and there was a tear in the ship's side. The water came in quickly and soon began to flood the compartment. Barrett moved back to No. 5 section, immediately astern, and could see that water was coming in there too, though he was sure there was nothing any further beyond this. This was still a long way back in the ship though and suggested serious damage had been done.

Barrett only just managed to get through the watertight doors, automatically closed by the officers on the bridge, in time. He could see that the empty coal bunker immediately behind the door was rapidly filling with water. The order was given for all men to stand by their stations, which meant to return to their posts. When Barrett went back to No. 6 section, climbing up a ladder and along to do so, it was impossible to carry out the instruction for it was already under 8 feet of water. This was within about ten minutes from the time of collision.

There were a few parts of the ship where people were well aware that something serious had happened. Those in the bowels of the ship, in the engine room and the boiler rooms could feel, hear and all too often see the effects of the collision. Those third-class passengers who were forward in the ship knew too because of their proximity to the accident.

But elsewhere on the *Titanic* reaction to the crash was muted. Some had felt a slight shaking – as if the ship was running over marbles, as someone put it – whilst experienced hands suspected that the ship had dropped a propeller blade. This had happened to the *Olympic* previously when she had struck a submerged wreck and would not have been welcome news as it meant that the *Titanic* would have to return to Belfast to get it fixed. That would have been most inconvenient. Still, if those aboard had known of the far worse alternative that was now unavoidable, they would happily have settled for that.

Many others were not initially aware that anything was wrong at all. Some slept soundly on as if nothing had happened. However, this state of affairs could not last long. What was more immediately obvious than what was happening was what was not happening. The ship had stopped moving. After five days of largely uninterrupted movement, the absence of the gentle vibration that had always been there when the ship was moving was odd. It was ironic that it was speed that had first caused the problem that had doomed the *Titanic*. Now it was the absence of any speed at all that alerted many to the fact that something was badly amiss.

5

CONSTRUCTION & DESIGN

A minute after the collision Captain Smith came rushing out of his room onto the bridge. He asked Murdoch what had happened. Murdoch replied, 'An iceberg, sir.' Smith ordered him to close the watertight doors at once. Murdoch replied that he had already done so, having activated the automatic closing of the bottom-most layer of them (amounting to some twelve doors in total) from the bridge by pulling a lever. They would shut within thirty seconds of the automatic closing device being activated. Made of heavy iron to the latest design, they should certainly hold the water back for a while.

The closing of the watertight doors would have been preceded by warning alarm bells ringing, giving the men just a few seconds to escape horizontally into the next compartment, though they could escape vertically by ladder if this option was no longer open to them. Once closed, the doors could only be opened manually and individually. If the doors should not for any reason shut when water broke in, there was a fail-safe device using floats that would close them once they came into contact with water. Higher up in the ship the watertight doors had to be closed manually. There is evidence that some of them at least were not closed and there certainly seems to have been no coherent system on board to ensure that they were.

Murdoch and Smith walked out on to the starboard wing of the bridge in an attempt to see the berg, but it had disappeared into the darkness. Boxhall went down below to try and see the damage. He walked along the passageway of the low-down F Deck but he could find no sign of any flooding. He made his way up to C Deck and then outside by the area where the berg had struck the ship. He returned to the bridge and gave Smith his seemingly good news.

Smith, however, wanted formal confirmation of the extent of the damage to the ship by a more thorough review. He therefore instructed that the order should be given to the carpenter to go and sound the ship – that is, to inspect the lower decks and assess how critical the collision had been regarding her integrity.

The carpenter was ahead of the game – he had already gone and done so without being asked. He was on his way up when he met Boxhall, who was looking for him. The carpenter asked him where the captain was. Boxhall told him and then asked if he had identified any serious damage. The reply was far from encouraging – the ship was 'making water fast'.

Whilst the carpenter proceeded to give Smith the grim news, Boxhall went to see for himself. On the way down, he met a mail clerk. He was also on his way to

Smith to tell him that the mail room, in the bowels of the ship, was filling with water. Arriving on G Deck and looking down, Boxhall could see that the mail room was already flooded and he could see water just a couple of feet away from the top of the ladder. It would soon be on G Deck itself. A despondent Boxhall could see mail bags floating on the water. There was nothing he could do down here and so he made his way back up to the bridge.

On board the ship, as part of the 'guarantee group' which had come out from Harland & Wolff to deal with any snagging issues that might arise, was Thomas Andrews, the shipyard's managing director and the chief designer of the ship. A supremely conscientious, hard-working and thorough individual, he was effectively the master architect behind the *Titanic*. If anyone knew how serious the damage was, it was he. So far his trip had been a hard-working but essentially mundane one and, being something of a perfectionist, all that had concerned him was a list of small adjustments to be made at a later stage. Now things had taken on a very different complexion.

Shortly after the collision, James Johnson – a first-class steward – was in the Saloon when Andrews walked through on his way down to the engine room. Smith did the same soon afterwards. Johnson followed Andrews down as he made his way to the mail room. Johnson could see the flooding and realised well enough that it was a 'bit serious'. Soon after, Andrews returned to the upper decks where he was seen reassuring a group of first-class ladies that it would be 'alright'.

Above: 1. The *Titanic* nearly strikes the *New York* as she leaves Southampton: the near miss suggested something of the difficulties of manoeuvring a ship this big.

Right: 2. The grand staircase, up which many first-class passengers made their way to the boat deck.

3. A famous picture (not a photograph) of a heavily illuminated *Titanic* at Cherbourg. Defenders of Captain Lord on the *Californian* say that it would be difficult to mistake a ship this distinctive.

Opposite: 4. A cut-away cross section of *Titanic* striking the berg: in reality the damage was less severe than this picture might indicate – but still more than enough to sink the ship.

Above: 5. A view of the crow's nest, from which lookout Fred Fleet first saw the berg – but too late. Below it is the forecastle of the *Titanic*, the first part of the deck to dip below the waterline.

6. The sheer scale of the *Titanic* can be seen in this photograph of her near-identical twin, *Olympic*.

7. The rear starboard boat deck and the second-class promenade area from which some of the second-class passengers boarded the boats.

8. Promenade deck 'A' from which some of the first-class female passengers boarded the boats.

9. A good photo of the *Olympic* illustrates the deck structure of the monster ships well and hints at the problems of segregation. In the top left corner you can see lifeboat 16.

Next page spread, left: 10. An illustration from 1912 showing *Titanic* striking the berg: the large submerged shelf of ice is speculative.

Next page spread, right: 11. Sketch of *Titanic* striking the berg: showing the berg scraping along the side.

Marconi Wires

1st Point of Contact with Ice

helf

Chart House

Bridge

4 Forward Boats

Submerged shelf

Boat Deck

4 Stern Boats

Starboard side

Direction of Iceberg after contact

First Class   Lounge   Promenade

Corridor   Private Suite   Promenade

Bath Rooms

First Class   Dining   Saloon

Companionway Stairs   Second Class   ←— Starboard port holes

Third Class   Dining   Saloon

ICEBERG
From 50 to 100 feet
according to various
accounts

Water Line

Boiler Room

Above left & centre: 12a & b. Bandmaster Wallace Hartley & cellist J. Wesley Woodward. Legends like that of the band can disguise the true horror of the catastrophe.
Above right: 14. Captain E. J. Smith, whose actions contributed significantly to the sinking.

Above left: 13. Illustration of *Titanic* sinking: the timing is wrong but the suggestion that she broke as she sank is not.
Above right: 17. A 1912 vintage wireless shack, similar to the one in which Phillips and Bride worked away tirelessly during the sinking.

Above left: 15. Second Officer Lightoller, heavily and controversially involved in loading the boats, who almost miraculously survived.
Above right: 16. Guglielmo Marconi, whose invention contributed to the preserving of many of those lives that were saved.

18. A romanticised view of the front promenade deck 'A' boats being loaded: in reality on one side of the ship first-class men entered the boats without any obstacle and no iceberg could be seen in the background as the great ship went down.

Right: 19. A crowded boat deck and a packed boat about to be lowered: however some boats went away only half full.
Following page spread: 20. The final moments approach – the bow dips under and there is not long to go for the masses trapped at the stern of the ship.

"The Titanic looked enormous"

Boat Deck clear of boats

"The bows & bridge completely under water"

"Sea calm as a pond
There was just a gentle heave"

"The starlight night was b[...]

Stern
2nd class
Section o[...]

"Every porthole & saloon was blazing with light"

Opposite: 21. The
final denouement:
the *Titanic* about to
disappear to the world
below.
Above: 22. Boats
approach the rescue
ship, *Carpathia*.
Right: 23. A fanciful
view of the *Titanic*
about to sink: by this
stage, she was torn in
two.

STERN
(Rear)

Above: 24. Plan of boat deck with the lifeboat numbers marked.
Left: 25. The real tragedy of the *Titanic* was in the story of survivors and the relatives of those who were lost.
Below: 26. First Officer William Murdoch.

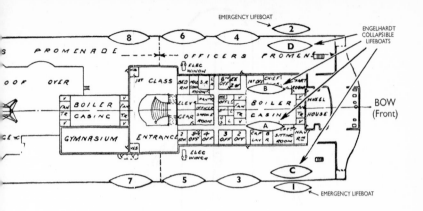

27. The *Titanic* being towed down Belfast Lough on her sea trials: unfortunately these were nowhere close to being comprehensive enough

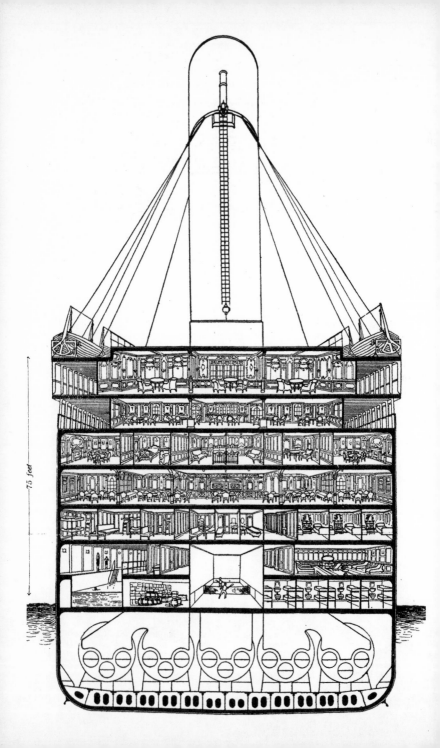

Opposite: 28. Cross-section of *Titanic*.
Above: 29. The opulent first-class smoking room on the *Titanic*: far more attention was paid to design features like this than to the lifeboats.
Right: 30. The rush to get to the boats. In reality, many third-class passengers did not reach the boat deck until there were very few boats left on it.

—*Detroit News*

EVERYTHING FOR ENJOYING LIFE, BUT NOT MUCH TO SAVE IT

Opposite: 31. Lowering the lifeboats: the drop down the side of the ship was so steep that for some it was a terrifying experience.
Above: 32. An ironic contemporary comment on the priorities on the *Titanic*, from an American newspaper.
Right: 33. A vivid view of the terrible fate of the *Titanic*.

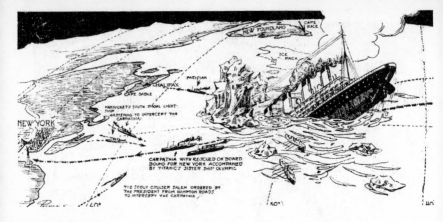

34. A newspaper's view of the ships in the area when the *Titanic* sank. The question on everyone's lips afterwards was 'was anyone close enough to help?'

35. Heroes till the end – the wireless operators at their posts until the last minute; however their actions earlier in the evening may have contributed to the disaster.

36. A boat approaching the *Carpathia*. Possibly number 6, one of the many that did not go back to pick up more survivors even though there was plenty of spare capacity to do so.

37. Collapsible boat D: lowering two of these boats proved virtually impossible due to the ridiculous position in which they were placed.

Above Left: 38. A towering iceberg in the vicinity of the wreck: an impressive but terrifying sight to the survivors.
Above right: 40. An injured Harold Bride, one of the two wireless operators on the *Titanic*, being helped ashore in New York after the sinking.

39. A huddled group of survivors on board the *Carpathia*.

Above left: 41. A picture of Jack Phillips, the wireless operator who did not survive the sinking.

Above right: 43. Survivor Margaret Brown presents a cup in thanks for the rescue of her and her fellow passengers by Captain Rostron.

42. Bruce Ismay being subjected to questioning at the American enquiry after the sinking (he is the man in the centre with the moustache). Many pointing accusing fingers at his part in the sinking afterwards, though without much solid evidence to back them up.

44. The bridge of *Titanic*.

Left: 45. A picture of the elegant *Titanic* sailing down Southampton Water on 10 April 1912.
Below left: 46. A biting commentary on the dangers of sailing too fast at sea.
Below: 47. Colonel Archibald Gracie, who made an amazing escape from the wreck, sadly only to die of ill health within the year.

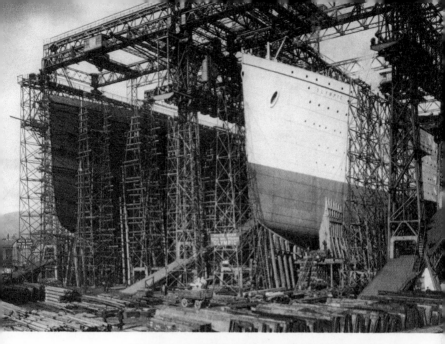

Above: 48. *Titanic* and her older sister *Olympic* on the blocks in Belfast. *Right*: 49. View of the stern and rudder: it was suggested in some quarters that the rudder was too small for a ship this big.

Above: 50. A view of *Titanic*'s huge propellers whilst the ship was being built in Belfast.

Below: 51. An interesting depiction of the relative sizes of the ship and the berg that sank her.

Opposite: 52. A picture from the *Sphere* showing ships in the area when *Titanic* sank: note that there is another ship between the *Californian* and the doomed liner.

The TITANIC WAS **175** FEET ABOVE WATER LINE

The ICEBERG INTO WHICH SHE CRASHED WAS ABOUT **100** FT AT THE HIGHEST PEAK

The TITANIC WAS **882** FT IN LENGTH

The LENGTH OF THE BERG IS ESTIMATED TO BE **500** FT.

The TITANIC WAS ABOUT **40** FT BELOW WATER LINE

The ICEBERG WAS BETWEEN **500** AND **700** FEET DEEP BELOW WATER LINE

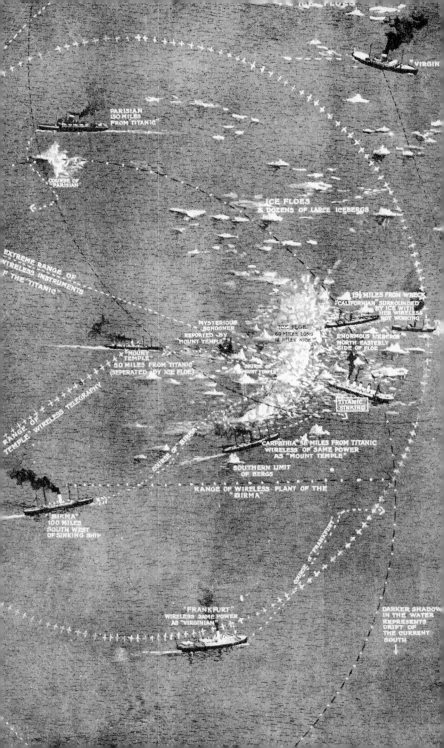

"VIRGIN"

PARISIAN
150 MILES
FROM TITANIC

COURSE OF
PARISIAN

ICE FLOES
& DOZENS OF LARGE ICEBERGS

EXTREME RANGE OF
WIRELESS INSTRUMENTS
OF THE "TITANIC"

19½ MILES FROM WRECK
"CALIFORNIAN" SURROUNDED
BY ICE WITH
HER WIRELESS
NOT WORKING

MYSTERIOUS
SCHOONER
REPORTED BY
MOUNT TEMPLE

ICE FLOE
60 MILES LONG
12 MILES WIDE

ENORMOUS ICEBERGS
NORTH EASTERLY
SIDE OF FLOE

"MOUNT
TEMPLE"
50 MILES FROM TITANIC
(SEPERATED BY ICE FLOE)

COURSE OF
MOUNT TEMPLE

TITANIC
SINKING

RANGE OF
TEMPLE WIRELESS TELEGRAPHY

COURSE OF BIRMA

"CARPATHIA" 56 MILES FROM TITANIC
WIRELESS OF SAME POWER
AS "MOUNT TEMPLE"

SOUTHERN LIMIT
OF BERGS

RANGE OF WIRELESS PLANT OF THE
"BIRMA"

"BIRMA"
100 MILES
SOUTH WEST
OF SINKING SHIP

COURSE OF FRANKFURT

"FRANKFURT"
WIRELESS SAME POWER
AS "VIRGINIAN"

DARKER SHADOW
IN THE WATER
REPRESENTS
DRIFT OF
THE CURRENT
SOUTH

Below: 53. The wireless station at Cape Race which did its best to assist with rescue efforts.

Right: 54. Captain Smith looks out from the bridge of his great liner, from where he would look in vain for the iceberg on the night of 14 April when it had disappeared into the darkness.

Below: 55. A contemporary cartoon showing 'women and children first'. This did not explain why so many women and children from third-class perished.

Right: 56. Horrified survivors look on whilst doomed passengers throw themselves off the sinking ship.

Above left: 57. A terrible fate. A doomed couple prepare to meet their end.
Above right: 58. Women were forced to row the boats in the absence of enough men in some of them to do so.

59. A newspaper breaks the news to a shocked world. The number of dead is about right: the number of saved women and children is far too high.

Left: 60. Distraught relatives and friends try to discover if their loved ones are safe from the White Star offices in Southampton where lists of survivors were posted outside. *Below*: 62. Longitudinal section of *Titanic*.

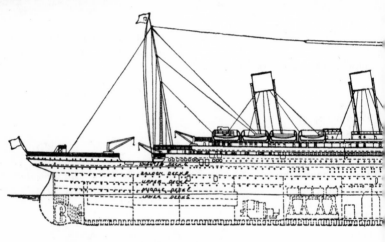

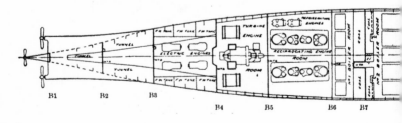

Right: 61. *Carpathia* drops off recovered *Titanic* lifeboats in New York. *Bottom of page*: 63. Tank top plan of *Titanic*.

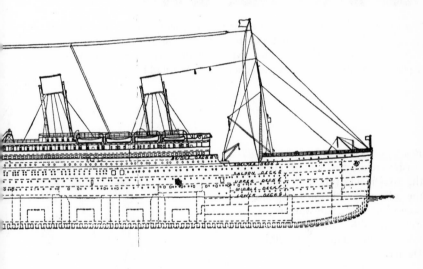

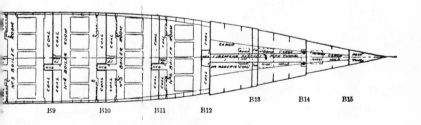

Above left: 64. Fred Fleet, the first man to see the berg. Fleet lived a tragic life even though he survived, and took his own life half a century later.
Above right: 65. P. A. S. Franklin, IMM Vice-President, who refused to believe early reports that the pride of his company's fleet had been lost.

Below: 66. Thomas Andrews the master architect of *Titanic*. He made the assessment of the ship following the collision and handed Captain Smith *Titanic*'s death warrant.
Below right: 67. *Titanic*'s lifeboats lowering mechanism, the Welin Davits.

Annie Robinson, a first-class stewardess, saw Smith and Andrews returning from their inspection of the mail room. They had also seen the squash court, by now filling up with water. Although Andrews seems to have kept his cards close to his chest, presumably in order to avoid a panic, his quiet instructions to Robinson shortly afterwards to put her lifejacket on suggests that he knew full well how serious things were. She did not at first wish to comply, feeling that the lifejacket looked 'rather mean'. The polite but firm reply was 'if you value your life, put your belt on'. Robinson should have known anyway; she had already seen the carpenter returning from his mission, looking 'absolutely bewildered, distracted'. As a result of these discreet inspections below decks, it was likely that Andrews had handed Smith *Titanic*'s death warrant.

The first six compartments of the *Titanic* had been opened to the sea: the Forepeak, Nos 1, 2 and 3 Cargo Holds and Nos 5 and 6 Boiler Rooms. Thomas Andrews, who knew the ship better than anyone, would not survive the sinking but his assistant, Edward Wilding, would be called to give evidence at the London enquiry held after the disaster. Wilding would calculate that the damage must have covered 249 feet, ending just a couple of feet inside No. 5 Boiler Room. However, the length of time it would take the *Titanic* to sink, two hours and forty minutes, meant that there could not have been a continuous gash, as some assumed would be necessary to wreck such a massive ship, but rather intermittent damage across that long distance.

Wilding calculated that the total aggregate damage could not have exceeded 12 square feet. The discovery of the wreck by Dr Robert Ballard in 1985 revealed something very interesting. Ships built in 1912 relied on rivets rather than welded plates and the *Titanic* had 3 million of them. Underwater exploration revealed that, rather than a massive gash, the seams of the riveted plates had 'popped' out as a result of the collision. Therefore the clash with the ice had forced some of the plates apart with the result that a number of leaks, rather than a huge tear, sank the ship. This is consistent with the view of Frederick Barrett that the water came in more like the flow from a fire hose than a raging torrent. Other surveys have led to suggestions that the rivets were of substandard quality, contributing to the disaster; but, as the sample sizes that these conclusions were based on were tiny, there remains considerable doubt that this was the case.

The nature of the damage though was decisive. Any four compartments could have been damaged and the ship would still have stayed afloat. She might have even hung on with the first five flooded. But six was just too many. The ship was now doomed. Water was pouring in, possibly at a rate of up to 7 tons per second. The pressure was huge and the front compartments started to fill up rapidly. This pulled the ship down deeper by the head. The problem was that the watertight bulkheads only went so far up the ship. As the water filled up the front compartments, it would eventually lap over the top of the bulkhead and into the next supposedly 'watertight' compartment. This would carry on until the whole ship was pulled under by the weight of water in the forward compartments.

The problem was that, when the ship was designed, no one had envisaged a worst-case scenario such as that which fatally damaged the *Titanic*. The worst that would happen in the normal chain of events was a smash at the joint of two watertight compartments which would end up with both of them being flooded. This left a considerable margin of error when up to four could be flooded before the integrity of the ship was compromised.

Similarly, the ship also had a double bottom which meant it could sustain damage there too and survive. The reality of course is that the 'unsinkable ship' cannot be built. A contemporary of the *Titanic*, the *Lusitania*, was partly financed by the British government as an armed merchant cruiser. Special attention was paid to her watertight arrangements, yet she sunk in just eighteen minutes after being struck by a torpedo in 1915. The year after, the *Titanic*'s younger sister, *Britannic*, was also lost after striking a mine in the Aegean (though some have suggested that the ship was carrying munitions and was sabotaged, but that is another story) – this despite the fact that the *Britannic* had been significantly modified after the *Titanic* disaster, with her watertight compartments extended.

Titanic had fifteen vertical bulkheads along her length, effectively dividing her into sixteen compartments which could, in theory, be isolated from each other in the event of water getting in. They were specifically strengthened to withstand the internal pressure of water building up in the compartments next to them should the ship be damaged. However, they did not extend all the way up the ship, going up as far as either D or E Deck. There were many openings and hatchways through which the water could rise and as a result lap over into the next watertight compartment, progressively pulling the ship down by the bow. Effectively, *Titanic* had no watertight tops to the compartments so that the water could just spill over from one to the next.

The double bottom, which stretched the whole length of the ship apart from a small portion at either end, also extended 7 feet up the side of the ship. It was later suggested that if it had been extended higher the ship might not have sunk. Another theory advanced was that if the ship had been divided with longitudinal as well as horizontally arrayed bulkheads then she would also have been saved (the effect would have been an internal design not dissimilar to a giant ice-cube tray). Both might have worked, although it is possible that the berg might have damaged the inner as well as the outer skin on the double bottom. However, longitudinal bulkheads were not a panacea as, if badly designed, they could cause one side of a ship to fill with water and not the other, eventually turning the vessel over.

A number of engineers were convinced that there were structural flaws in the design of the *Titanic*. An article in the *New York Times* of 12 May 1912 compared the ship unfavourably with her contemporary competitor, the *Mauretania*, and even the *Great Eastern*, Brunel's ship which had sailed the oceans half a century before (though it is noticeable that such know-it-all opinions were much less in evidence before the disaster). The latter had longitudinal bulkheads that were carried right up to the upper deck (these effectively gave her fifty different watertight compartments – such measures came at a cost which was not merely financial; it made it much more difficult for the crew to move from one part of the ship to another, for example). She once managed to survive a collision with a rock that left an 80-foot tear in her outer skin.

In any event the damage to the *Titanic* was, the London enquiry concluded, done at about 10 feet above the keel. Within ten minutes in most affected areas the water level inside the ship had risen by 4 feet. It continued to fill at an alarming rate and there was no way that the ship could be saved.

No story of the *Titanic* would be complete without a brief discussion of the 'unsinkable' tag. It has often been pointed out that the White Star Line never said any such thing about the ship, but actually they and others came pretty close to doing so. This is important, as it helps to explain the attitude towards safety that prevailed on the ship. White Star marketing material produced in September 1910 said of the *Olympic* and *Titanic* that 'these two wonderful vessels are designed to be unsinkable'. That is certainly helping to create an impression that she was. The month after, the *New York Times* suggested that the *Olympic* and the *Titanic* would be 'practically unsinkable and absolutely unburnable'.

In 1911, the *Shipbuilder* magazine, a trade publication rather than an item of marketing material, said that

each [watertight] door is held in the open position by a suitable friction clutch, which can be instantly released by means of a powerful electro-magnet controlled from the captain's bridge, so that in the event of accident, or at any time when it may be considered advisable, the captain can, by simply moving an electric switch, instantly close the doors throughout and make the vessel practically unsinkable.

Well, the watertight doors had been shut with the electric switch and yet there was the great ship slowly but inexorably sinking.

Even the prudent Captain Rostron of the *Carpathia* said that

> the ships are built nowadays to be practically unsinkable, and each ship is supposed to be a lifeboat in itself. The boats are merely supposed to be put on as a standby. The ships are supposed to be built, and the naval architects say they are, unsinkable under certain conditions.

It is not quite clear what 'unsinkable under certain conditions' means. A ship is either unsinkable or it isn't.

It is also worth considering the comments of Philip Franklin, vice-president of IMM and as such just about as senior a figure as there was amongst the company that owned *Titanic*. When he later broke the terrible news in New York that she had indeed gone, he told the press reporters listening incredulously to his statement that 'I thought her unsinkable and I based my opinion on the best expert advice. I do not understand it.' Well, if he didn't, it is perhaps unsurprising that ordinary passengers could not understand it either.

The fact that, even after the event, people could not quite accept that the *Titanic* had sunk, shows how much observers were impressed by the sheer size of the ship as well as her safety arrangements (which were, incidentally, superior to many other ships of the day). This superiority added to the sense of invulnerability perhaps felt by many responsible for the safety of the *Titanic*.

There was one quote in particular which stood out with regard to the sinking. It was this:

I cannot imagine any condition which would cause a ship to founder. I cannot conceive of any vital disaster happening to this vessel. Modern shipbuilding has gone beyond that.

And who said this? It was the master of the *Adriatic* after completing her maiden voyage in 1907. His name? Captain E. J. Smith. Now Smith was presiding over a nightmare of incredible proportions. He had made another off-the-cuff remark in that earlier newspaper article, that he was 'not very good material for a story'. Well, he was certainly headed for the headlines now.

There were pumps on the ship and for a while some hoped that they would succeed in keeping the situation under control – one who thought they might (or at least said so at the time) was Chief Engineer Joseph Bell. At one stage extra pumps would be put into No. 4 Section in the Boiler Room, which had not been affected by the original damage, to try and keep the water out – but it did not work.

Sometime later, Boxhall asked Smith how serious the damage was. The reply was that Andrews gave her an hour to an hour and a half to live. However, Trimmer Samuel Hemming had heard the same message second-hand and recalled hearing it only ten minutes after the collision (he also thought that he had said 'half an hour to live', which would have been a very pessimistic assessment). That said, it was clear that at an early stage Andrews knew that the ship was doomed.

Most of the men down below had gone up onto the deck when the ship started to fill with water, but Barrett remained down in No. 5 Section. Although the bunker at the forward part of this was flooded, the stokehold itself remained dry. He remained there with three other engineers. Then the lights went out, so Barrett sent some men back to the engine room to collect some lamps. Ironically, shortly after they returned, the lights came back on again and would remain on in parts of the ship until very close to the end.

Soon after, a number of men came down to the stokehold to make sure that the fires in the boilers stayed out; the fear was that if they did not then if the boilers were flooded an explosion would ensue and quicken the ship's end. They took about twenty minutes to do this and went back up again. Barrett was left on his own along with Herbert Harvey and Jonathan Shepherd, both engineers. Unfortunately, Shepherd failed to notice an open manhole, fell down it and broke his leg.

Another fifteen minutes passed and No. 5 Section stayed dry. The ship though was noticeably starting to tip, that is to say there was an increasing slant forward. Suddenly, without warning, there was a rush of water down a passageway which quickly started to flood No. 5 Section. Although Barrett could not be sure, it was as if one of the watertight bulkheads had given way under immense pressure (though in all probability it was the weaker door of the coal bunker which gave way when the bunker itself filled with water). Barrett scrambled up a ladder to get away from the flood; sadly both Shepherd and Harvey would not survive.

One of the horrors of the disaster was that it unfolded so slowly. There was so little obvious damage noticed by many people immediately after the collision that some passengers were very slow to try and board a lifeboat (though this was not true of everyone). Only gradually did it become clear that the ship was sinking, as the deck began to tip beneath their feet. For many, it was only the deafening sound of escaping steam from the ship's funnels and the fact that the great liner was stationary in the water that alerted them to ominously changed conditions.

But not all were in this category. Archibald Gracie was a first-class passenger who would survive the sinking in very dramatic circumstances. When *Titanic* finally went under, he went with her. However, he managed to get to the surface and scramble onto an upturned collapsible boat which served, not very comfortably or effectively, as a form of raft. He would write a book about his eventful journey and in it he told how he had decided to investigate for himself after the collision and soon found out that the mail room was flooded. Not long after, he and his friend 'Clinch' Smith noticed a definite list on the ship. He suspected from very early on that the *Titanic* was in serious trouble. Despite this, he bravely made no attempt to save himself and became one of those heroic first-class men around whom the *Titanic* legend would be built (out of 175 first-class men, 57 survived – so clearly not all of them were part of this legend).

Second Officer Lightoller would later on play a key role in loading the lifeboats. He had his own way of gauging how quickly the ship was sinking. He monitored the rate by every so often going to check on one of the stairways that led down below. Each time he looked, another step or two had disappeared.

Stewardess Violet Jessop had a different way of seeing how the ship was slowly sinking. She got away in a lifeboat and could see the ship, lit up almost as if nothing at all was wrong. She had always wanted to see the ship at night. Now she could, but it was a most strange sight indeed. For the bow of the ship was underwater and sagging ever deeper. The rows of lights she could see from the portholes were the strangest of all, for she watched, in horrified fascination, as one by one they disappeared beneath the surface.

This was quite late on in the process. At 1.35 a.m. the forecastle deck was not underwater but ten minutes later it was. After that, the rate of sinking increased rapidly. Water started to rush up onto the deck, creating chaos in its wake. Clearly the massive weight of water in the flooded areas of the ship was tugging it down ever quicker.

The end arrived at 2.18 a.m. The *Titanic*'s bows had now disappeared far under the water. The stern of the ship was pulled into the air in what seemed to many eyewitnesses a perpendicular position. She was like a finger pointed to the sky, a beautiful but disturbing sight beneath the backdrop of the inky black night, lit only fitfully by the pinpricks of light that were coming from the stars. Her huge propellers were raised helplessly in the air, high above the level of the water that they were supposed to be driving the ship through.

At this point, the stresses on the ship became too great. She had of course never been built to cope with being in such a horribly distorted position. At some point between the third and fourth funnels she snapped in two – the official position in 1912 was that this was not the case but, given eyewitness accounts and the discovery of the wreck in 1985, that view is almost certainly wrong. One of the funnels broke off and fell into the water, killing some of those who were already in the water but unwittingly saving the lives of others when the wake from the crash pushed them towards some of the collapsible boats that were in the proximity of the dying ship. Just before this point, the lights had gone off, come back on for a second with a flash and then went out forever, adding further to the sense of terror that must by now have been overwhelming for those still left on the *Titanic*.

Then, at the last, she slipped almost quietly under the waves, out of the world of man and into the lost abysses of the ocean, eventually ending up (in bits) on the sea floor over 12,000 feet below. At 2.20 a.m. she was gone. Despite the fears of many, the suction was almost unnoticeable: one man, Baker Charles Joughin (fortified by a large tot of alcohol), hardly got his head wet as he stepped off the disappearing stern rail into the sea.

The dream had been five years in the making and had been destroyed in under three hours. A catastrophic denouement had been a strong possibility since the ship, forearmed with a number of warnings, had sailed at not far off her top speed into the death zone. But once the lookouts had failed to spot the ice in time, the nature of the collision made the *Titanic*'s sinking unavoidable. Her design had not envisaged a collision of the nature that would sink the ship or the extent of the damage it would cause. As soon as the ice was struck in the way it was, *Titanic*'s demise was a mathematical certainty.

But that only told part of the story. There had been nearly three hours between collision and sinking. Plenty of time to get everyone safely loaded onto a lifeboat from a slowly sinking ship. Plenty of time too for nearby ships to come and rescue survivors. Yet the incontrovertible fact was that, come the cold light of day, over 1,500 dead bodies would be drifting in the North Atlantic or trapped in a rusting tomb at the bottom of the ocean. And the only ship that did come to the rescue would arrive nearly two hours after the ship had sunk. Both outcomes, it would transpire, were a long way from being merely bad luck.

6

THE BOAT PROBLEM

The chain reaction was complete. The *Titanic* was now doomed. However, that was not the end of the story. Far from it. It is now considered normal practice to have in place emergency procedures by which, in such a situation, most – or hopefully all – of the passengers and crew get off alive. The fact that it is now normal practice is in part because of the *Titanic*. The importance of the disaster is not in the dramatic story and the immortal legends, gripping though they are. It lies much more in the changes that were made because of the catastrophe. After it many people realised that things could simply not go on as before.

Another chain reaction now comes into play, that which led to the loss of 1,500 lives. Given the amount of time that there was to abandon the ship in an organised fashion, there was no need for anyone, or at most a few, to be lost. How then did the massive loss of life ensue? To this we must turn to other considerations, namely:

- The situation with the lifeboats.

- The response of nearby ships.

- The response of those in the lifeboats once they had reached the water.

In examining these three considerations, we will come across the most controversial issues of all those concerning the disaster.

The issue of the lifeboats is a complicated one, for there were in fact a string of related events all of their own which led to such a large loss of life. These were the lack of lifeboat capacity, where the lifeboats were positioned on the ship, the lack of any real pre-planning for an emergency evacuation, and the way that the lifeboats were loaded (these last two factors are to a substantial extent cause and effect). In analysing these areas we will come across several fundamental and ultimately fatal failings, in particular a stunning sense of complacency and a complete breakdown in organisation when it could least be afforded.

Most people are well aware that the *Titanic* had insufficient lifeboat capacity for all those on board. That this is demonstrably true will be fully illustrated shortly. But this is only a part of the story. It would be wrong to think that, with lifeboats on board for everyone, most of the lives of both passengers and crew would be saved. That simply cannot be true. Otherwise how can it be explained that there was room for 500 more people in the lifeboats that were actually launched, or that even as the ship was starting to disappear into the ocean depths all the available boats had not yet been launched?

The reason for this lies at the heart of the tragedy of the *Titanic* – a shipping company that completely failed its passengers and would, in a modern world, in all probability be facing a charge of corporate manslaughter. But was this alone responsible for the complete lack of a plan of action in a crisis on board the *Titanic* that night, or the fact that the White Star Line's most senior and valued officer was completely overwhelmed by the nightmare situation that was unfolding, unbelievably, slowly but inevitably, as if in slow motion, before him?

On board the ship were fourteen full-size elmwood lifeboats (30 feet long, 9 feet broad, 4 feet deep) with a capacity of around sixty-five people. There were two smaller emergency boats (about 25 feet long, 7 feet broad, 3 feet deep) which could take about forty people each. In addition, there were four collapsible boats which could carry forty-seven each. These were boats with pull-up sides that could be fitted into the davits from which the other lifeboats had already been launched and then lowered away with more passengers. Such at least was the nice and simple theory. The practice was somewhat different. Two of the four collapsibles were stowed on top of the roof of the officers' quarters. They weighed several tons and there were no cranes to lower them to the Boat Deck below. It would prove next to impossible to launch them when the sinking ship was burrowing at a crazy angle into the sea. It was as if no one had ever expected them to be needed.

The total capacity of these boats in aggregate was 1,178 people. The London enquiry stated that 2,201 people were aboard. Although the passenger manifests and crew lists were subject to some error and *Titanic* historians may argue about a few individuals who they feel were aboard but were not listed (or vice-versa), it follows that there was not enough boat room for over 1,000 people on board. The *Titanic*'s maximum capacity for passengers and crew was 3,547 people so it was just as well that she was only 60 per cent full, otherwise the death toll could have topped 2,800.

How did this seemingly indefensible position come about? There were several reasons for it. Firstly there was the fact that the regulations concerning lifeboat capacity were very old and frankly had been left lagging far behind as technology moved forward (or so it seemed) at an incredible rate of knots. In order to sail, a passenger ship had to get a licence from the British Board of Trade, which regulated amongst other matters the issue of lifeboats. They were totally out of touch with what was required given the rapid expansion in ship sizes in recent years. Accusations of 'old fogeyism' were well founded.

That increase in size had been made at an incredible pace. White Star was often at the forefront of such increases, earning a reputation for launching a number of 'largest ships in the world'. One of them, the *Cedric*, had been launched in 1903. At the time it was suggested that it was not possible to build a bigger ship. Its size? 21,000 tons – less than half the 46,000 tons of the *Titanic*. Perhaps after all there was no limit to the size of ships and, by definition, to man's ingenuity and power. It was also interesting that the *Cedric*, because of its safety features, was also described when first she sailed as 'practically unsinkable' by the *New York Times* – a phrase that would ring a few bells in 1912.

One witness to the London enquiry was Sir Alfred Chambers, the recently retired Chief Adviser to the Board. The regulations for lifeboats dated back to 1894. Chalmers had been asked from time to time whether they needed changing. He considered that they did not. His reasoning was confused to say the least. There had been no major accidents in recent years – it was 'the safest mode of travel in the world' (three major disasters in four years, namely the *Titanic*, the *Empress of Ireland* and the *Lusitania*, each with the loss of more than 1,000 lives, would challenge this assessment fundamentally – however, to put this in context, out of 6 million passengers carried across the Atlantic between 1902 and 1911 there had only been seventy-three lives lost). Also as ships got bigger, they also got stronger. More lifeboats than the *Titanic* had would 'encumber the decks unduly' (presumably interfering with first-class passengers promenading around the deck, and also blocking their view).

Other matters that Chalmers thought pertinent included the fact that ships now carried wireless, that they sailed along agreed shipping lanes – making collision less likely – and that more lifeboats would require more crew to be carried. Breathtakingly, he considered that even after the *Titanic* disaster, more boats should not be carried as it would be impossible for the captain and crew to cope with them all. To add to the impression that Chalmers was living in some kind of parallel universe, he further suggested that having fewer lifeboats would not result in any fewer lives being lost. His reasoning was that the passengers, seeing there were few boats available, would pile onto the boats in large numbers, avoiding the situation such as occurred on 14 April 1912 when boats went away half full (this did not have an awful lot to do with the passengers but rather with the amateurish way in which the boats were loaded).

For some strange reason, the logic of which is best known to those who introduced the provisions back in the nineteenth century (officials tried to explain the reasons to the court of enquiry in London but only seemed to have confused their listeners and made themselves look rather silly in the process), the number of lifeboats required was based on the gross tonnage of the ship rather than the number of passengers that she carried. In fairness, when one reads the transcripts, it seems that some of those examining witnesses at the London enquiry found it equally difficult to work out this byzantine logic.

Put simply, the regulations on lifeboat capacity in place at the time were related to the tonnage of the ship. Up to a figure of 10,000 tons, there was a relationship between the size of the ship and the lifeboat capacity. It was when the tonnage exceeded 10,000 tons that the relationship went askew. Above this figure, there was a minimum lifeboat capacity that was prescribed which was fixed regardless of the ship's size. There was, beyond this 10,000-ton benchmark, no relationship between the size of the ship and the lifeboat capacity. A ship of 15,000 tons was legally required to carry the same number of lifeboats as one of 45,000 tons.

This was because, when the rules were brought in, the largest ship was covered by this 10,000-ton limit. But in the two decades since, they had increased in size almost by a factor of five. The *Titanic* ironically was not only operating within the rules with her lifeboat capacity but was actually providing more boat space than she legally needed to. In reality, virtually every large ship, whatever flag she sailed under, did not have enough lifeboat space for a large number of the people on board. As one example, the German liner *President Lincoln*, also built by Harland & Wolff, could carry 4,108 people but only had lifeboat space for 1,465 of them. To sum up the stupidity of the situation, the *Carpathia*, which came to the rescue of *Titanic* survivors, carried eighteen boats, only two less than the superliner even though *Carpathia* was less than a third of *Titanic*'s gross tonnage and could carry less than half her passengers.

Still, some of the senior figures in the British shipping industry continued to argue, even post-*Titanic*, that no change was needed. Harold Sanderson, the managing director of the White Star Line, was one such. He felt that in most cases it would be impossible to lower all the boats safely anyway and persisted in this view even after the *Titanic* had sunk. The magazine *Fairplay* told its readers that those on board 'could avoid all these [problems] by drowning at once'.

Others wanted to take measures after the disaster to increase the 'flotability' of the ships rather than the lifeboat capacity. They obviously thought that ships could be made even more 'practically unsinkable' than *Titanic* was but, as the modified *Britannic* showed, you cannot make an unsinkable ship. In fact, these individuals showed themselves completely out of touch with public opinion and soon after shipping lines would voluntarily ensure boats for all. The *Titanic* had made that inevitable.

Resistance to change came from out-of-touch officials. But the clamour for change was irresistible. When the *Olympic* was about to sail on her next voyage from Southampton soon after the sinking, her crew refused to do so unless there were boats for all on board. When one of those provided was found to be substandard, the shipping line ended up with a non-violent mutiny on its hands. Legally the men were indeed mutineers and they were taken to court as such. They were found guilty but the court refused to impose any meaningful sanctions on them, this clearly being a case where it wished to apply the spirit rather than the letter of the law. There was nothing for it; White Star provided boats for all long before there was any actual change in the law. It was so clear in the light of the disaster that it was nonsensical not to do so that the company backed down pretty much without a fight.

The supreme irony was that *Titanic* had been equipped with technology that could have easily provided a lifeboat space for everybody on board. Alexander Carlisle had been general manager of Harland & Wolff when *Titanic* was being built (though he had left the company before she was finished). He was involved with the design of the ship and in particular the lifeboats. Special davits had been used which would allow four boats to be stored in each position, meaning that there would be room in a boat for everybody aboard, even when *Titanic* was full.

Carlisle had put his ideas forward to the Welin's Quadrant Davit Company and they had come up with the appropriate design. This had been done, not particularly because of any eye to safety considerations, but because the Board of Trade were (in 1909, when these discussions took place) reviewing their regulations and it was thought possible that they might increase their requirements. In the event this did not happen. The designs were submitted to a senior official of the White Star Line for discussion – J. Bruce Ismay. When the Board of Trade did not increase the lifeboat capacity requirements, the plan to have four lifeboats in each position instead of one was quietly dropped.

The advisory committee appointed to look into the number of lifeboats to be carried had reported back in 1911 and had actually recommended that the regulations be changed so there was less, rather than more, lifeboat capacity available. It was only by good fortune that the changes had not been enacted when the *Titanic* disaster took place. One of the members of the committee who signed off the recommendations was the selfsame Alexander Carlisle, who admitted that 'I was very soft the day I signed that'.

For those lifeboats that were on the *Titanic*, nearly all of them were positioned on the Boat Deck, which also served as a promenading area for first-class passengers. With it being right next to some of the more luxurious first-class cabins (there was not really any such thing as a 'standard' first-class cabin – some of them were indeed palatial), it meant that it was very easy for first-class passengers to access the boats quickly in an emergency.

This was also the situation with second-class passengers. There were some boats in the second-class promenade area (though it would do little good for the male second-class passengers, who suffered the highest mortality rate of any category on board) but there were none at all in third-class areas. This was a particular problem as there was active segregation between different areas on the ship and first- and second-class sections were out of bounds to third-class passengers. As the Boat Deck was in a first-class area, this was a major issue.

There were a number of barriers on the ship preventing access of the third-class passengers to the Boat Deck. Some crew members would say after the disaster that there was no attempt to stop them from accessing the boats as the ship was sinking. However, the evidence of those third-class passengers who survived starkly contradicts this view. Some of them only lived because they took matters into their own hands and ignored instructions to stay where they were; there were accounts after the sinking of some of them climbing up cranes as makeshift ladders to get up to the boats. Others were dragged (or climbed) out of the water after the ship sank.

There were a few examples of stewards leading parties of women and children up from third-class to the Boat Deck. That they needed to be led at all is indicative of several problems – partly that they would not have known their way up to the Boat Deck because they had never been there before and partly because there were physical barriers to stop them doing so which needed to be manoeuvred around.

There were many accounts in newspaper articles after the tragedy suggesting that there was little systematic attempt at official levels to get to the bottom of the problem. The London enquiry for example stated that there was no evidence of discrimination against third-class passengers. There was a good reason for this – those involved in the enquiry did not bother to look properly. Instead they decided that the reason for the high number of losses in third class was that they were too attached to their few possessions and did not want to abandon them.

There was plenty of evidence there for those who wished to look. There was, for example, the story of Kathy Gilnagh, who was held back at a barrier with her friends by a crew member. In this case, the actions of one of her male companions, who bellowed at the crew member, did the trick. Another third-class passenger, Annie Kelly, told that most of her class were stopped from coming up until the last moment. Margaret Murphy said that the doors were locked leading up from third-class. Male passengers were shouting at the sailors and fighting broke out. Seaman John Poingdestre saw a hundred men waiting with baggage beside a ladder to second-class which was blocked by stewards. Charlotte Collyer saw guards positioned to stop more passengers from coming up on deck.

One senior official tried out for himself after the disaster on the *Olympic* how long it would take to move from the third-class accommodation areas to the Boat Deck. The longest time he took was three and a half minutes, which shows that there were obstructions placed in the way of passengers down below in third-class areas who were taking so much longer to make the journey. Colonel Archibald Gracie was shocked when, with the last boats already gone, suddenly appearing from below decks there was 'a mass of humanity several lines deep, covering the Boat Deck, facing us, and completely blocking our passage towards the stern'. There were no barriers strong enough to hold them back now but it was far too late to matter.

Another survivor of the sinking was third-class passenger Olaus Abelseth, who was part of a small group that also included his sister. He told how they had been kept away from the Boat Deck until late on. The women had then been let up but the men had still been kept down. When they at last arrived, virtually all the boats had gone. It was extraordinary that he survived, another of those who, managing to escape from the ship as it sank into the darkness of the world below, got onto one of the collapsible boats.

It is not easy to determine whether this was conscious or unconscious discrimination. Were so many third-class passengers ignored as part of an active decision to ignore them or just through oversight? In the end it is does not really matter; the evidence shows conclusively that in the scheme of things they simply did not count. Even at the time not everyone was taken in by the myth of universal male heroism and 'women and children first'. The London *Daily Herald* produced a cartoon of a pompous-looking first-class passenger floating on a life raft in the shape of a coffin with the number 134 engraved on it. The caption beneath stated that 'fifty-eight "men" of the first-class were saved; one hundred and thirty-four steerage [third-class] women and children were lost'.

The situation was no doubt compounded by the complete absence of any scheme to load the boats properly as the disaster unfolded. The problem started with the lack of any clear boat drill in preparation beforehand. Fifth Officer Harold Lowe was given the responsibility of checking the boats out in Belfast before *Titanic* set sail for Southampton, along with Officers Boxhall, Pitman and Moody. This was more an inspection than anything else, checking that the oars, rowlocks, sails, rigging and other gear were all present. The boats were also required to carry a compass, water, biscuits, a light and oil though when these items were needed not everybody was able to locate what should have been there.

Before *Titanic* left Southampton a token trial of the lifeboats was held under the presumably watchful eye of Captain Maurice Clarke of the Board of Trade, who was to confirm that all the safety arrangements were in order before the ship could leave. Two boats were lowered away from the side of the *Titanic* with their crews and rowed around the docks for twenty minutes or so. The crews were then hauled back on board and went off to their breakfasts before returning to their daily tasks. No other activity that could be remotely construed as a boat drill was held on the *Titanic* between the departure from Southampton and the time that the ship struck the iceberg. Unfortunately, this lack of practice and preparation was to show itself with shocking effect when it was most needed.

The interview at the London enquiry with Captain Clarke was very interesting indeed. He admitted that after the disaster the pre-sailing checks had been significantly tightened. The interview went as follows:

'Did you think your system was satisfactory before the Titanic disaster?'

'No, sir.'

'Then why did you do it?'

'Because it was the custom.'

'Do you follow a custom because it is bad?'

'Well, I am a civil servant sir, and custom guides us a good bit.'

It was of course a shocking admission but it would do to describe many aspects of the disaster. Why did captains sail full speed in known ice zones? Because custom had guided them. And why were there not enough lifeboats on board? Again, because of custom. But it was not just custom; it was the lack of any terrible example to hold before any of the guilty parties. They all did these things because in the past they had always got away with them. Not anymore. All this would now change.

There was also evidence of stunning complacency in the lack of any meaningful arrangements for lifeboat drill. There was supposed to be a minimum of two seamen per boat if the lifeboats ever needed to be launched and yet the tests at Southampton involved only sixteen people. Steward Edward Wheelton later explained that it was not possible to have a full boat drill before leaving Southampton as this would have interfered with getting lunch ready for the passengers who would soon be boarding – an interesting insight into priorities on the new superliner. Quartermaster Hichens explained that he had been accustomed to taking part in a lifeboat drill on every Saturday when he had been on other ships (others remembered that it was normally on a Sunday). No such drill had taken place on the *Titanic*.

Given the lack of organisation, when the *Titanic* was involved in its fatal collision no one really knew where to go. For example, Fireman George Beauchamp made his way up from far below but he had no idea where he was headed. There had been a list assigning crew to boats that morning – or so he had been told – but he had not seen it. He had looked for one earlier in the voyage but there had been none there to see. Robert Hichens also made his way to a boat, but which one it was he could not remember. He admitted that he did not really know what boat he should have been on, but that was not surprising as he had not been involved in any boat drill since he had been on the *Titanic*. He also had not seen the list with the lifeboat stations on it.

This would prove a particular problem when the boats started to be loaded. It was just after 12.30 a.m. that the boats on the *Titanic* started to be filled. There was at first little sense of urgency. The only one who seemed concerned to lower the boats quickly was Ismay. He urged haste on the officers loading them even before any official orders were given to put people in the boats. He first of all approached Third Officer Pitman and encouraged him to put women and children in. Pitman did not recognise Ismay and went to check with Captain Smith on whether he should comply or not.

Shortly afterwards Second Officer Lightoller was involved in a similar discussion with Ismay. Once again, Lightoller was not sure what to do so he went to check things out with Smith as well. The upshot was that shortly afterwards the instruction to start loading the boats with women and children was put into effect.

This was a rather surprising turn of events. Ismay presumably knew how dire the prognosis was because he was obviously anxious to get the lifeboat-loading process under way as quickly as possible. He was therefore apparently fully briefed on the dangerous predicament that *Titanic* now found herself in. The same could not be said of two of the senior officers on the ship, who had clearly not been told anything by their captain. Even when the boats started to be loaded, they were still little the wiser; when asked why he did not put more people in the first boats away, Lightoller protested that is was 'because I did not know it was urgent then'.

There was still not much of a rush to get in them though. A number of officers took charge of loading the boats, with First Officer Murdoch prominent on the starboard side and Lightoller on the port, though other officers were also involved. An interesting difference in approach soon became apparent. Murdoch interpreted his instructions to be 'women and children first' which meant that, if there were any spaces, men were freely allowed in. Lightoller on the other hand took his orders to mean 'women and children only' which meant some boats went away half full (or worse). Given the fact that there was not enough room to go around as it was, this seemed foolish.

Part of the problem, so those responsible for the loading argued, was that they were unsure how many the boats could safely carry when being loaded to the waterline. They were afraid that putting too many people in the boats would cause them to buckle in the middle. But the lifeboats had been tested in Belfast on 25 March and had been safely lowered into the water with seventy people in them. This vital information was clearly not passed on to any of the *Titanic*'s officers, who seemed totally in the dark as to how many each boat could safely hold when being lowered the 60 feet to the water.

It was not quite clear why this was so. It is possible that no one had briefed Captain Smith, though not to pass on such a crucial piece of information would seem incredible if it were not for some of the other sloppiness around at the time. But it is also possible that Smith did not pass it on, as for a time he seems to have lost his nerve when faced with the awful situation. It was as if the whole terrible drama was too much for him to cope with. It is notable that Lightoller insisted that until quite late on, 'I did not think ... the ship was going down'. As the Second Officer of the ship – and one of the men loading the boats – it is impossible to work out why he had not been given this rather important item of information.

Smith in fact exhibited some very muddle-headed thinking during these admittedly agonising moments of crisis. At one stage, he even forgot the layout of his own ship. He decided that Boat 4 should be lowered from A Deck, one down from the Boat Deck, and this was duly done. But then someone remembered that, unlike the *Olympic*, where it was open, on the *Titanic* it was enclosed, so Lightoller – in charge of loading the boat – brought the boat back up again. But then he thought that it could be loaded from A Deck if the windows were opened, so back down she went. Those who were trying to board her were understandably pretty peeved by the time that this fiasco concluded.

One witness to this confusing scene was first-class passenger Hugh Woolner. It was he who reminded Smith that, unlike the *Olympic*, A Deck was enclosed and that this plan was not therefore a very good one. 'By God, you are right!' was Smith's response. Given this belated realisation, it is not at all clear why it was decided that Boat 4 would eventually be loaded from A Deck anyway. It was a piece of time-wasting complication when it could be least afforded.

Understandable though it is from a human perspective, it was a terrible time for Smith to be so out of touch. His calm demeanour could have been a strength in ensuring that the lifeboats were coolly loaded with as many passengers as possible. He would have known better than most how short of lifeboats his ship was, a situation for which he personally could not be blamed. However, where he was open to criticism was in now failing to take control of the loading of the boats, a deficiency which led to the loss of nearly 500 lives that could otherwise have been saved.

This led to some extraordinary events. Lightoller lowered away one boat before he discovered that there was only one man in it to row. He therefore called for a volunteer. Major Peuchen, a Canadian who was an experienced yachtsman, put himself forward. The lifeboat was already part lowered so the only way he could get in was to climb down a rope. Lightoller said that if he could do it, then he could go and Peuchen duly obliged.

The failure to designate seamen systematically to the boats, allied to the absence of a boat drill, could have resulted in further catastrophe. In several instances there was a danger that one boat would accidentally be loaded on top of another. One lifeboat was nearly swamped by the overspill from the pumps. In others, women passengers told of having to row because there were no seamen in the boats capable of doing so. In truth, it was a shambles.

This was certainly also true of the numbers put in the boats. The worst example was that of the Emergency Boat (No. 1), which had a capacity of forty but was lowered with twelve in it. However, plenty of others were almost as bad. Major Peuchen was baffled by the policy. He noted that 'every woman on the port side was given an opportunity. In fact, we had not enough women to put into the boats. We were looking for them. I cannot understand why we did not take some men. The boats would have held more.'

The fact that the boats went away with spaces because there were not enough women on the Boat Deck tells its own story. The reason that there were no more women (or children) there to load was because many of those in third class were a long way away from the Boat Deck. Otherwise if it really were women and children first, then why did so many from third class die? Of the adult females in third class only 76 out of 165 were saved. For children it was even worse with only 27 out of 79 surviving. But if they were not around to be saved then why at least not try to save male lives? As Stoker Walter Hurst, looking on, remarked, 'if they are sending the boats away, they might as well put some people in them'.

As the night went on, the sense of urgency increased. When the order was first given to load the lifeboats and hand out the lifebelts, the commutator was already measuring a significant list to starboard. There were 3,560 lifebelts on board, spread across the sleeping quarters, and it seems that most people who wanted one got one when they needed it. As the ship sank deeper, the tilt became more noticeable. For those down below, the reality of the situation became clearer too when the water started to fill up the lower decks where many of them were berthed. Then, as rockets were shot off to attract attention, it was also obvious that the problem was a serious one.

Despite this, there were clearly issues with the way that people were being directed up to the Boat Deck even as the boats were running out. Bruce Ismay stepped off in the last boat to be properly launched and was much castigated for his actions in surviving when so many of his passengers died. Yet, he insisted, no others could be seen around the boat to get on. With over 1,500 people condemned to die, it raises the question 'Where were they?' Yet as the ship was about to take her final plunge, Second Officer Lightoller had looked around him and saw those selfsame missing people in a 'dreadful huddled mass' and thought to himself 'how fatal it would be to get amongst those hundreds and hundreds of people'. It appeared that people were being stopped from getting close to the Boat Deck but were allowed to make their way to the stern, which was not normally a prohibited area for third-class passengers.

For those who did get through to the boats, the pace of loading got quicker as the situation worsened, more passengers were put in and more wanted to go. It became apparent to everyone eventually that there were not enough boats to go round. What also did not help was the positioning of the collapsible boats. Two of them were adjacent to the boats on the Boat Deck and could therefore be put into the empty davits once the wooden lifeboats in them had been launched. However, the two on top of the officers' quarters were another matter altogether. Once they were the only two left, Second Officer Lightoller called for men to climb up and help him to get one of them down.

By this time, the situation was desperate. Water was starting to wash up the Boat Deck. Lightoller and other crew members cut away the ropes, hoping to have the chance to put the boat in the davits and be able to load her with those still seeking escape – but it was far too late. With the Boat Deck already dipping under, all that they could realistically hope for was that some would be able to climb aboard her when she was in the water.

It was of some help. The boat floated off the ship and was soon the target of dozens of desperate swimmers who sought safety of a sort on board. Some would find survival through it, but of course there would have been more if the boat could have been properly lowered away. Colonel Gracie also helped cut away one of the collapsibles from the top of the officers' quarters. The plan was to lower it down to the deck on some oars that had been propped up against the structure but it was far too heavy and it crashed to the deck.

Wireless operator Harold Bride was watching, having been relieved of his duties in the shack. He looked on as a dozen or so men were trying to lower the collapsible onto the Boat Deck and were clearly struggling to do so. He decided he would help them. Even as he moved to do so, a wave rushed up the deck and carried the boat off it. Bride would be one of those who owed his life to the badly launched collapsibles. He would spend the next few hours sitting in water in the improperly launched boat after he managed to climb aboard it from the water. He would suffer severe frostbite to his feet but would recover.

The truth was of course that these boats should never have been in such an inaccessible position in the first place. It showed a terrible lack of planning, but like so many aspects of the disaster this was not through incompetence as much as complacency. The White Star Line were able to demonstrate that they had complied with the rules as far as lifeboat requirements were concerned and that was after all another piece of positive publicity that they could show to the travelling public they wished to woo. They of course deserved to be criticised after the event for their complacent and cavalier attitude towards safety. The same was also true – if not even more so – for the body that was supposed to be regulating them.

But this just said everything there was to say about the loss of the *Titanic*. The boat situation summed up everything that was wrong with the regulation of the shipping lines and their own attitudes to safety. There was a great irony in all of this, one of the greatest myths of all about this tragic ship and its tragic life and death. The myth is that lifeboats for all on board the ship would have saved everybody's life.

The evidence does not bear this out. Given the fact that there were still boats not properly launched when the ship dipped under, how would those on board have managed to get everybody off safely without a major change in the way that things were done? For a start, it was the best part of an hour after the iceberg was struck before the loading of the boats commenced. Whilst it was natural and sensible for Captain Smith to avoid a panic and not load the boats until he was aware of how serious the damage to his ship was, it is hard to believe that he did not know some time before this – especially as it was not him who appears to have initiated the process but rather Ismay through talking to some of Smith's other officers.

Then there was the fact that the boats went away half empty, certainly early on. Even if there had been four times as many lifeboats on board, sending them away only half full would still have meant that lives would have needlessly been lost. The lack of a lifeboat drill was also a major problem, with seamen not designated to help load specific boats or assist with the rowing of them. With more lifeboats, the sense of chaos would, without any proper lifeboat drills, have merely increased. When twenty boats could not be loaded properly and efficiently in an hour and a half, what chance would there have been of loading so many more in the same time? And of course if third-class passengers in particular were not properly directed and led to the Boat Deck in good time, then it would have made very little difference to them how many lifeboats were on board the ship.

All of these detailed points underline a greater truth; the loss of life on the *Titanic* was so great because no one – or at least not the right people – took the issue of safety seriously. They could not conceive of any situation in which the boats might be needed, other than to go to the assistance of some smaller ship that was in trouble and help to take its crew and passengers off. (What, someone wondered, would have happened if the *Titanic* had caught fire? Then lifeboats for all might well be needed, even if the ship was really in all other respects unsinkable). It was a significant though ironic reality that if the *Olympic* had arrived on the scene in time to pick up survivors (she received the wirelessed SOS but was too far away to help), there would not have been enough lifeboat space between the boats of the two White Star superliners combined for all the people that were on the *Titanic* in need of rescue.

That was the truth about this tragic situation; no one believed that this ship could sink. She was her own lifeboat and even in the aftermath of the situation – stark and unarguable as it was – the so-called 'experts' continued to argue that the issue was not of more lifeboats but of making the ships even more 'unsinkable'. This also spoke tellingly of the mindset of those involved; nature could be conquered, bested by man, tamed and controlled. Even in the face of the evidence that a large block of ice could send mankind's proudest achievement to the bottom of the ocean in less than three hours, still there were those who defied reality and refused to face up to the truth that no ship is unsinkable.

7

The Other Ships

Not long after the collision, when the extent of the damage was starting to dawn on him with horrifying clarity, Captain Smith made his way to the wireless shack, telling Jack Phillips to send out the call for help. It must have seemed unbelievable to the wireless operator that such a summons needed to be made but he got to it at once. The plea for aid went across the airwaves. Phillips hoped that there would be someone close enough and awake enough to hear it.

What happened next is largely the story of two wireless men: Harold Cottam on the Cunard ship *Carpathia* and Cyril Evans on the closer *Californian*. It was only by luck that Cottam was up at all. He had been waiting for some messages to arrive and they had not yet come in. Getting tired and frustrated, he was about to turn in. However, he had some messages from Cape Race for the *Titanic*; mundane matters, not anything of particular importance, but he thought he would pass them on.

So he wirelessed *Titanic* to do so, expecting to enter into some small talk with the operator on board the magnificent new liner. Before he could do so, however, Phillips urgently interrupted. 'Come at once, we have struck a berg' was the simple but shocking message. Cottam could barely believe his ears and asked Phillips if he wished him to alert his captain. Phillips affirmed that he should. It was about 12.30 a.m. *Carpathia* time and it would turn out that the ship would not be able to reach *Titanic*'s reported position for nearly four hours.

Captain Arthur Rostron of the *Carpathia* had turned in for the night. A man who liked discipline, he was rather put out when Cottam came bursting into his cabin with the First Officer. However, his mind was quickly turned to other things when the stunning news was given to him. He ordered the ship to be turned round, then he asked Cottam if he was sure that his information was correct. That was Rostron's way – to act decisively when the occasion demanded.

The situation could not have been more different on the *Californian*. Cyril Evans had turned in at 11.30 p.m. *Californian* time. That was no cause for criticism. He ran a one-man show on the ship and he needed to sleep at some point. It was a quiet night, the ship was stopped and going nowhere and he had dutifully relayed a warning of ice to the *Titanic*, which could not be far away – not that she seemed particularly interested in such information. There seemed little to do, so he decided to call it a day.

However, that was not the end of the story. At 12.15 a.m., Third Officer Groves came into the shack. He was on good terms with Evans and fancied himself as an amateur wireless operator. He put on the earphones and listened intently to see if he could pick anything up and, if he could, whether he could make any sense of it. But there was nothing. He did not realise that the power had died. He put down the phones, turned out the light and left the room. At just about the same time, Phillips was sending out his first distress call.

If luck, Fate or the Hand of God played any part at all in the loss of the *Titanic*, it was in this missed opportunity to pick up the message summoning aid. In the absence of 24-hour wireless cover it was all a matter of luck when an operator was working and when he was not. Evans's blameless decision to turn in at 11.30 p.m. led to a lost chance to save 1,500 lives.

But that was not the end of it from the *Californian*'s perspective. Far from it. Whilst Lord – also at this stage blameless as his ship was stopped and he had done his job in sighting the ice and bringing her safely to a halt – dozed off, the bridge was in the hands of Herbert Stone. He was on watch from midnight to 4 a.m. Stationary as they were in the North Atlantic on a quiet, dark night, it should have been just about as routine a watch as he could get. But in fact it would turn out to be one of the most dramatic watches in maritime history.

Before Lord had turned in, he had pointed out the lights of another steamer to Stone. The Second Officer thought that they were about 5 miles away. He kept an eye on it, not for any particular reason but just because it was there. But then he thought he saw a white flash above the steamer. At first he thought it might be a shooting star but then he saw four more flashes in succession, white rockets coming at three- or four-minute intervals. Eventually he decided to report them to Captain Lord at about 1.10 a.m.

Lord's voice came through from the other end of the speaking tube from the bridge to his room. He asked Stone if he thought what he had seen were company signals – recognition signals that ships fired off from time to time. But Lord did not seem unduly bothered by them, so Stone returned to his watch, where he was joined by apprentice James Gibson. They then watched together as three more rockets went up.

There then followed perhaps one of the most bizarre conversations in maritime history. Gibson remarked that a ship would not be firing up rockets at night for nothing. Stone was not concerned, for his captain seemed to think they were company signals (which was a strange assumption for either man to make, as Lord had not actually seen them for himself). But Stone thought something else was odd about the rockets; they did not appear to be very high, almost as if they were coming from behind the ship that they could see from the *Californian*. He also could not hear anything – and rockets were supposed to make a very loud bang when they exploded – which may again have helped persuade him that they were not distress signals.

The two men looked on at the curious stranger. At one stage Stone thought the lights of the ship looked odd. They remarked to each other that the ship looked 'queer'. Gibson thought that she looked as if she had a 'big side out of the water'. He thought it looked as if she had a list to starboard. So, as eight rockets went up in close succession, the two men continued to watch a ship whose lights looked odd and which gave the impression she might be listing. Despite what Stone in particular said later, they must surely have suspected that there was something wrong. But they did nothing.

Another witness would also come forward from the *Californian* to say that he too had been looking on. His name was Ernest Gill and he was a 'donkey man' – a quaint way of saying that he worked in the engine room. He went out on deck twice for a cigarette. The first time he saw the nearby ship. In his view she

> could not have been anything but a passenger boat – she was too large. I could see two rows of lights which I took to be porthole lights and several groups of lights which I took to be saloon and deck lights. I knew it was a passenger boat. That is all I saw of the ship … She was a good distance off I should say no more than ten miles and probably less.

He would later go out again and this time he saw rockets going up (though he could not see a ship by now, which was strange as those watching from the bridge could). Although he said he wondered why no one was doing anything, he did not consider that it was his job to report the rockets as they must have been able to see them from the bridge and, basically, it was none of his business. This was a rather cavalier attitude from Gill and he did not always come across as a credible witness. He was also paid by a newspaper for his original story, which does not make him a liar but does give him an ulterior motive for telling the story. Despite these doubts, however, his story added to the suggestion that there was a pretty slipshod attitude aboard the *Californian* that night.

Why the men on the bridge did nothing is a question that will never be properly answered. It calls into question the nature of their relationship with their captain. They did eventually decide to talk further to Lord, first of all at 2 a.m. when Stone sent Gibson down to the captain, and then at 2.40 a.m. when Stone talked down the speaking tube to him. At 2 a.m., Gibson reported to Lord that the other ship was 'disappearing' – Stone insisted it was steaming away – to which the captain asked whether there were any colours in the rockets, the last of which had been seen twenty minutes before the report was made: Lord's argument being that the presence or otherwise of colours in the signals could indicate if they were indeed company recognition signals.

The suggestion that they might have been company signals is not at all a convincing one. Lightoller not so subtly suggested what he thought of Captain Lord's (in)actions when he told the London enquiry, 'there is no ship allowed on the high seas to fire a rocket or anything resembling a rocket unless she requires assistance'. He further twisted the knife when asked if he would have recognised the meaning of the signals if he had seen them from another ship; the unequivocal reply was 'I have seen them, and known immediately'.

Second-class passenger Lawrence Beesley produced a well-written account of the disaster and described the scene when the rockets first shot up and exploded into a cascade of stars in the air:

> ... and then an explosion that seemed to split the silent night in two,
> and a shower of stars sank down and went out one by one. And with

a gasping sigh one word escaped the lips of the crowd: 'Rockets'.
Anybody knows what rockets at sea mean.

Well, apparently, not quite anybody.

At 2.40 a.m., Stone reported via the speaking tube that the mystery ship had gone. At least, he said he did. The strange thing was that Lord remembered neither this conversation nor the one at 2 a.m. It is true that when Gibson entered his room on the earlier occasion, his report suggested that Lord was half-asleep. The speaking tube though was harder to explain away as Lord would have had to have got up from the couch where he was napping and walked across the cabin before he had what appeared to be a coherent conversation with Stone in his sleep before forgetting all about it.

This was of course extraordinary, though it was made more extraordinary because these men were apparently unwitting witnesses to the greatest shipwreck in history whilst all this inactivity was not going on. Eight signals were seen and the nearby ship looked odd. But nobody did anything about it. Most extraordinary of all was the lack of a decision to wake up Cyril Evans, the wireless operator. He could have been on air again in five minutes, the ship going in a few minutes more and who knows what might have happened then?

It is hard to avoid several conclusions. The first of them was that the men on the bridge were showing an incredible amount of apathy in what appeared to them to be a weird situation. Stone's inability to be more decisive suggests both character weaknesses and a far from healthy relationship between a captain and one of his senior officers. It was a shame in retrospect that it was not Chief Officer George Stewart on the watch as it was he who would rouse Cyril Evans first thing in the morning to find out what had gone on – but then it was far too late.

What was particularly heartrending about all this was the fact that witness after witness who survived the sinking of the *Titanic* spoke of the lights they could see from another ship when they were sinking. Fourth Officer Boxhall was busy starting to load the boats when someone reported seeing a light from the bridge. It looked to him like the two masthead lights of a steamer. At one stage, she appeared to be approaching the *Titanic* and Boxhall believed her to be a four-masted steamer. When she was close enough, Boxhall used the Morse lamp to try and communicate with her. Someone thought they could see a response back but they could not be sure. Boxhall thought she was about 5 to 6 miles away but then she seemed to slowly turn round until all they could see was her stern light. It must have been agonisingly frustrating but it eventually became clear that whatever ship was there was not coming to help.

Lightoller could also see a light from a ship in the distance. In contrast to Boxhall, he thought that the vessel he could see was perfectly stationary. This would also be circumstantial evidence against the *Californian*, for she was in such a state, though her head did move around slightly during the night because of the current's drift. Third Officer Pitman could also see the light and thought that it was motionless. Fifth Officer Lowe saw the lights on several occasions an hour apart and was sure that they were in the same place every time, whilst lookout Fred Fleet also thought they never moved.

But Quartermaster Hichens thought that the light was 'moving, gradually disappearing'.

So there was no consensus amongst the witnesses from the *Titanic* about whether or not the light was moving. What there was a degree of consensus about was that a light could be seen and at one point apparently even Captain Smith suggested that the lifeboats should pull towards it. Indeed, a number of them did. But even that consensus was only partial. Some of the witnesses thought that the light was a star, others that it was the Northern Lights playing tricks with people's eyes. Even those who thought that it was indeed a light from a vessel of some sort could not agree on what it was, with some thinking that it was a steamer whilst others thought it only a trawler. But those who did try and pull for the elusive light had to give it up as a bad job by morning as they could make no progress towards it.

There was a major difference of opinion between Captain Lord and those who felt that he had been negligent in his actions as to exactly how far away the *Californian* was from the *Titanic*. Lord had written his position up in the log when he stopped and found out that he was over 19 miles away from the *Titanic*'s reported position when she struck the ice. It did not help that Boxhall, who calculated just what this position was, was some miles out in his calculation, though as its main effect was to make the *Titanic* further east than reported rather than north it did not make her materially closer to the *Californian*.

If the *Californian* was indeed 19 miles away from the *Titanic* then she could not have got there before the *Titanic* sank. It would take her well over an hour to steam there and if Lord had reacted to the rockets

reported at 1.10 a.m. *Titanic* would be well on her way
to the bottom of the ocean by the time she was on the
scene, if indeed she had not already landed on it. That
would have been too late for most of those in the water,
most of whom had lifebelts and did not drown but froze
to death. Life expectancy, given the fact that the water
was virtually at freezing point or just over, would be no
more than twenty minutes in most cases. Lord could
only in the main have recovered the dead.

However, not everyone accepted that he was 19 miles
away. Lord Mersey, who chaired the London enquiry,
was damning in his indictment of the *Californian* – and
in particular her captain – and simply refused to accept
that Lord was correct in his stated position. His chairing
of the enquiry left a lot to be desired. It is not that he
was necessarily wrong in his judgement of Lord and the
Californian. Because of his ineptitude we shall never know.
Having taken the trouble to call a number of witnesses
from the *Californian* (though by no means all who could
have been called) he decided far too early that Lord was
a guilty man. This meant that glaring contradictions in
witness statements – and there were many of them – were
simply not properly followed up until the inconsistencies
had been ironed out. This meant that those historians
who wish to build a case for or against Lord merely had
to select which pieces of evidence they wanted to support
their argument, and they have succeeded in writing a
number of books that do just this. In the absence of any
rigorous cross-examination of most of the witnesses, we
shall probably never get to the truth.

Yet whether or not Lord could have got there in time
is not the entire point anyway. The fact is that he did

not try. Why he did not react to the reports of rockets is mystifying. He knew as well as anyone that this was a dangerous night, otherwise why was his own ship stopped? He knew that a number of rockets had gone up and why after all would ships be sending off company recognition signals at one o'clock in the morning? It was a matter of minutes to wake the wireless operator and make sure and Lord does not come across as the kind of man to have been too bothered about the sensibilities of a relatively junior member of staff about having his beauty sleep disturbed.

Then there were the conversations he could not remember, those at 2 a.m. and 2.40 a.m. Why did he forget them? Was he exhausted? Although it would have been stressful being on alert for the ice, it does not otherwise have seemed to be a particularly taxing day. Unfortunately, Lord did (and does) not come over as a convincing witness. Neither does he seem a particularly warm one. When a story came out that there were suggestions that the captain of the *Mount Temple*, who was also in the area though further to the west, was tardy in coming to the rescue, Lord seized on it as a way of diverting attention elsewhere.

Certainly, it is hard to make sense of what was happening (and equally what was not happening) on the *Californian* that night without assuming that there was an uncomfortable relationship between Lord and the men who were on watch. They seemed almost fearful of taking the initiative by waking the wireless operator or by pushing Lord to react to the issue of the rockets: Stone after all had not even bothered to inform him until he had seen five of them. Then when he did report them he was content to rely on his captain's implied suspicion that they were not distress rockets, even though Lord had not seen them for himself. These were strange decisions indeed.

What a contrast with the *Carpathia*. As soon as he heard the news that the *Titanic* was in great danger, Rostron sprung into life, fully exhibiting that energy which would earn him the nickname 'the Electric Spark'. The list of instructions which he came up with on the spot was supremely impressive, especially given the nightmare scenario that lay before him. It seemed to cover almost every conceivable problem that might arise. Not only did it include all the obvious things, such as getting the ship up to speed as quickly as possible or preparing the lifeboats, but it also covered arrangements for feeding the survivors or finding somewhere for them to sleep and even having thick oil on hand to put down the lavatories in case the sea was rough.

No detail seemed too small. Rostron even ordered that the heating system be turned off to ensure that all available energy was being directed towards driving the engines at maximum speed. This would also have the beneficial side effect that the *Carpathia*'s own passengers would be encouraged to stay in bed; the last thing the captain needed was superfluous people getting in the way with a crisis situation to handle. Then Rostron, a deeply religious man, closed his eyes, uttered a prayer and sprang into action.

The *Carpathia*'s top speed was normally about 14 knots but she made 17½ that night. At about twenty minutes before three o'clock Rostron saw a green flare, the White Star line's signal, some way ahead. He hoped for a time that the *Titanic* was still afloat. This would have been surprising as the last wireless message, received an hour before, was that the 'engine room was full up to the boilers'. But just then the icebergs came into view too and Rostron was forced to weave in and out of them as well as he was able.

As Rostron sailed on determinedly towards the green light, from time to time he sent up a rocket as reassurance to whoever might be still alive that help was on the way as quickly as he was able to bring it. The passengers in the lifeboats could see the rockets go up and it understandably buoyed spirits as they knew that help was at hand, though few knew at this stage who from. These rockets were also seen by those on the bridge of the *Californian*. It is perhaps not in the least bit surprising that these signals were not reported to Captain Lord at all. Even though it was now gone three in the morning, no one on that ship seemed at all surprised to see the rockets continuing to shoot up into the sky.

It is of course undeniable that there was something wrong on the *Californian* that night. Even Captain Lord was forced to concede that there was 'a certain amount of slackness' aboard his ship, though it is not clear that the implied criticism extended to himself or his own particular management style, which seems to have inhibited any degree of initiative from his officers. But he insisted until the end of his life that his position as he wrote it down in the log was correct and that, unless someone could prove that he was mistaken or had 'cooked' the records, he would not be budging from his deeply held belief that it put him nearly 20 miles away from the *Titanic*. To support his view, other officers – in particular Chief Officer Stewart – had validated the position of the ship when she stopped for the night.

The British enquiry was having none of it. In its concluding report it stated definitively that the lights seen from the *Titanic* belonged to the *Californian*. Whilst admitting that there were inconsistencies, Mersey ignored them and concluded that the *Californian* was 8, or at the most 10, miles away. His main reason for doing so was that no other ships were reported in the area; therefore it had to be the *Californian*. In his view, if she had tried to come to the rescue, 'many if not all the lives that were lost' would have been saved.

Senator Smith, heading the US Senate enquiry, concurred that he thought that the *Californian* was much closer than 19 miles away. Lord's inaction was 'reprehensible' and failed to comply with 'the dictates of humanity, international useage [*sic*] and the requirements of law'. It was not clear whether this arose from the captain's 'indifference' or 'gross carelessness'.

It is difficult to absolve Lord of any blame for his failure to respond to the reports of rockets in the night in a known danger area for ice. However, it is important to point out that there would almost certainly have been other ships in the area that night. Indeed, there is incontrovertible evidence that there were. The evidence for this comes from Captain Moore of the Canadian Pacific steamer *Mount Temple*.

Moore's ship had received a wireless message saying that the *Titanic* was in trouble. He had turned his ship around and headed towards the sinking liner's reported position (which was wrong). At about three in the morning he saw a sailing vessel coming from the opposite direction – that is, where the *Titanic* had been. He estimated that this was about 16 miles away from where he believed the White Star ship to be. She was not moving very fast but he had to take evasive action to avoid getting too close to her. He also saw a small steamer of about 5,000 tons to the south of him during the night and believed that he could see her again in the morning, though he was unable to name her.

Then there was the strange story of the *Samson*. She was a small seal-hunting ship which regularly plied her trade in the icy vastness of the Arctic Ocean. She set sail on a voyage from Norway in February 1912 and made her way to the waters off Newfoundland. Hendrik Naess was a crewman, who claimed that he was out on deck on the night of 14 April when he saw bright lights away to the south. A lookout shouted that they were not stars, as originally thought, but lanterns. Then several rockets were seen shooting up. The crew of the sealer did nothing as they were sealing illegally. They saw nothing in the morning and slowly returned to their home port.

On their way back, they put into Iceland, where they heard for the first time of the loss of the *Titanic* and realised that they had been unknowingly watching her last hours. More recently, doubt has been cast on this story and there have been suggestions that it is just a good sailor's yarn as records show that the sealer was in port in Iceland at a time that would have been impossible, given her slow speed, if she was present when the *Titanic* sank. But other research has suggested that the dates involved were the dates that the sealer should have been in Iceland and not the dates she actually was.

Then there was the *Mount Temple* herself. After the sinking of the *Titanic*, witnesses came forward to say that rockets were seen by Captain Moore yet he did little to try and intervene. There were suggestions that his testimony to the two enquiries was inconsistent and that he was overcautious due to the presence of a large ice field. It was alleged that he was much closer to the *Titanic* than he admitted. In the rather sensationalist reporting of the day, one contemporary newspaper article alleged that she was so close that passengers on the *Mount Temple* could hear the creaking of chains on *Titanic* as well as the shrieks of terrified passengers.

Strange, sometimes inherently impossible, stories were a feature of the disaster. It was even said that one *Titanic* crewman was later brought on board the *Mount Temple*, something for which there is no corroborating evidence whatsoever. But suffice to say it would be unlikely that the *Californian* was the only vessel around that could have helped. These were popular fishing grounds too and there would likely have been trawlers in the vicinity.

But that of course does not exonerate Captain Lord from the fact that he did nothing, and the strange actions of his crew continued when day broke. The surreal chain of events on board the *Californian* continued when Chief Officer Stewart came back on the bridge. At four in the morning, when it was still dark, he put his binoculars to his eyes and picked up a steamer to the south. Second Officer Stone told him that he had never seen her before, so it was clearly not the ship that they had been watching during the night.

Half an hour later Stewart decided to rouse Lord. He told him that a number of rockets had been seen in the night. Lord came on the bridge and looked at the ship to the south. He said, 'She looks alright.' But, in keeping with the bizarre actions that had been going on all night, Stewart did not tell Lord that the ship he was looking at was not the one that had been seen during the hours of darkness. Yet more time passed in this strange charade before Stewart decided he would at last go and wake up the wireless operator. However, it was not, he said, because he feared that something had happened, but because he wished to know the identity of the ship to the south.

Cyril Evans was at last roused from his slumber. He picked up the phones and started to feel around the ether to see who he could pick up. It was a matter of minutes before he heard the astonishing news that the *Titanic* had sunk. He rushed up with the news to Lord on the bridge. A short time later, the *Californian* started to push her way gingerly through the ice. She nosed her way west, ironically through to the wrong side of the ice. Once she was through she made her way south, more quickly now that she was free of danger. She would later see the *Mount Temple*, also on the wrong side of the ice pack.

Then on the other side of the ice Lord saw another ship. He pushed his ship back again through the ice and moved closer to it. The *Californian* and the *Carpathia* were at last alongside each other. Rostron, who had picked up all the survivors he could find, moved off after asking Lord to look for anyone he had missed. The master of the *Californian* did so for a few hours and then also moved west towards the coast of America and the deceptive tranquillity of Boston, where his ship's carpenter would soon break the news to a disbelieving world that rockets had been seen from the bridge of the *Californian* on the night that the great ship went down but no one had done anything.

It is true that there were probably other vessels on the scene that night. In fact, it is almost certain that there were. But it is also true that no other ship reported seeing eight rockets fired off on the night of the world's greatest shipping disaster. Whatever his reasons, Lord of the *Californian* would never escape the suspicion that he might, just might, have made a difference if he had been quicker to respond to the telltale flares that illuminated the ebony blackness of the North Atlantic sky during the early hours of 15 April 1912. The debate started weeks after these epochal events occurred. It still rages on, with no sign of resolution, one hundred years later.

8

THE BOATS IN THE WATER

As the *Titanic* slipped beneath the surface and out of the sight of man for another seventy-three years, there were still hundreds of lives at stake. Some undoubtedly went down with the ship, trapped below and unable to get away from their terrible fate. Many though would have had plenty of chance to get up on deck. Indeed, reports from survivors speak of large numbers of people heading for the stern of the ship as she tipped lower into the water, Gracie's 'mass of humanity' hoping against hope for survival even at this late stage when it was clear that the ship herself was going down.

There were twenty boats in the water, including the two collapsibles that had not been properly assembled. There was room for nearly 500 more people in those boats. Yet at the end of it all only a handful of survivors were picked up from out of the water. This inevitably led to some suggestions that not everybody had behaved as heroically as they might have. But it was also, it seems, a departure from the original plan.

Lightoller for one suggested that he planned to put down the boats – he mentioned Boat 6 in particular – part loaded and they could then be loaded more fully when they were in the water. He even sent a party of seamen down to open a gangway door so that this plan could be facilitated. But in keeping with the generally amateurish lowering of the boats all night, he did not tell anyone on Boat 6 to stay close to the side of the ship. It was also equally tragically in keeping with the all-round incompetence that some of the gangway doors were at the front end of the ship – the end that was about to disappear under the water.

The plan was anyway to lower a rope ladder from the gangway to the lifeboat lurking helpfully just off the ship (the plan would have probably worked better if Lightoller had told the men manning the boats to take this action rather than hoping they used their initiative to work out they should do so – initiative seemingly being in generally short supply at that precise moment).

Later, Lightoller recalled seeing Captain Smith with a megaphone, ordering the boats to come back closer to the ship. Lightoller was busy loading boats at the time and could not see whether the order was being complied with, but it appears not. Lightoller also made an astonishing admission later, namely that he had not told the captain that he had ordered the gangway doors opened. The lack of coordination involved in the rather serious matter of getting as many people in the lifeboats as possible would have done justice to a Grand Guignol farce.

Boxhall was one of those who, from his boat in the water, heard the stentorian tones of Smith sounding out through the megaphone. He endeavoured to move back closer to the sagging ship (he had been ordered into Emergency Boat No. 2 and had manoeuvred off the ship by about 100 feet by this time). However, it proved very difficult for him to do so; there was a singular lack of men in the boat with any knowledge of how to row properly – again the lack of forethought about who should be deputed to what boat was revealing itself as a substantial problem. Boxhall was blessed with the grand total of precisely one seaman in his boat.

In any event, as the boat was close to the ship, Boxhall felt the effect of suction start to affect his small craft so he decided to move it further off. He eventually moved the boat until it was he guessed half a mile away from the now clearly doomed liner. Here he stood off for a while whilst he considered what to do next.

Another officer to get off was Fifth Officer Harold Lowe. Third Officer Herbert Pitman also escaped. But other officers, Smith, Wilde, Murdoch and Moody, all perished. It would have been useful to have had some of these men on the boats, one would think. They could in theory take control of the situation and bring a degree of organisation to the boats. Such might be the theory, though the practice of loading the boats in the first place might suggest a rather different and inefficient outcome would be the result.

Lightoller had found that when the ship went down she had disappeared from under him and he was pulled under too, being caught for a moment against a grating, the air rushing out of which created a suction effect that threatened to keep him below the water. But then he broke free and rose to the surface. He came up by the upturned collapsible boat he had been trying in vain to launch and hung on to the side. He eventually climbed aboard and recalled that about six others were on it. By morning, the number was up to thirty.

Some way off, Boxhall lit a light in the boat – his was one of the few that was so equipped – in an attempt to try and group the boats together. This was an advantage of having an officer in charge of the boats; a degree of coordination was welcome at a time like this. But the boats were too dispersed for this to happen.

When the ship went down – Boxhall was too far off to see it happen but was alerted that the denouement was imminent when the lights on the *Titanic* went out – he was made aware of the fact not by anything he could see but by the awful cries that rose up out of the frigid waters as hundreds of dying souls, their life being sucked from them by the icy sea, cried for mercy to their God or more practically to those in the boats that lay scattered around the death zone.

Boxhall debated whether or not to go back but in the end he decided not to do so. He said that there was only space for another three people in his boat. This is slightly surprising. Eighteen people were listed as being in his boat – in a craft that was meant for forty. In the aftermath of the disaster, many would say that there was no room in the boats to take anyone else on board, but time after time such statements would not be backed up by the facts.

The worst example was the other 'emergency cutter', Boat 1. This would be the most controversial boat of them all. This was lowered away with the sum total of twelve people in it. The most notable, or at least noticeable, of these were Sir Cosmo and Lady Lucy Duff Gordon. Their secretary, Laura Francatelli, was there too. In the aftermath of the sinking, whilst the boat waited for rescue, Lady Duff Gordon's greatest concern seemed to be that her secretary had lost a beautiful nightdress in the disaster.

It was a comment that understandably got some of the crewmen in the boat somewhat riled. They had lost their jobs and their kit – they were effectively unemployed from the moment that the ship dipped below the water. One of them made a comment about this, to which Sir Cosmo replied that he would give them £5 each for their losses. However, some did not accept this interpretation. To them it seemed like he was offering them money not to go back into the mass of humanity that was now struggling for survival in the water. From then on, Boat 1 would be known as the 'Money Boat'.

There was though, the evidence suggests, little or even no discussion in Boat 1 about going back at all (the evidence as with so many matters *Titanic* is not quite definitive on the point but the discussion that took place on the subject was at best brief). There was no forceful voice raised to insist that a boat with room for another twenty-eight people on it should go back and try to pick up some of those who were dying a few hundred yards off. Those on the boat did not raise a finger to help anyone.

Yet another example was Boat 6 – capacity 65, number on board 23. The man nominally in charge of this boat was Quartermaster Robert Hichens, the same man whose hand had been on the wheel when the *Titanic* fatally grazed the berg. There was a long and fierce debate with some of the mainly female occupants of the boat about whether or not they should go back to pick up survivors. It was alleged that Hichens said there was no point as there would only be 'stiffs' there now (though he denied that he ever said such a thing). But the end result, whatever was said, was that no one else was picked up by Boat 6.

The only man who seemed to have any moral fibre in this respect was Fifth Officer Lowe. Here was a man who was outspoken but determined and no respecter of authority. He had earlier on berated Bruce Ismay for trying to get him to load the boats more quickly and had also fired off several shots from his pistol when he thought there was a danger that the boats might be rushed as those left on the sinking ship had suddenly realised that the boats were running out.

Lowe was in charge of Boat 14, which was in the water some forty minutes before the *Titanic* went down. He stood off from the ship, like most others no doubt aware of the great suction that would occur when the *Titanic* went under. After she finally disappeared, and the terrible wailing of those seeking rescue had started to die down, he decided that he should try and pick up more survivors.

He summoned a group of boats in the vicinity together (this was what an officer should surely be doing in a time of crisis: taking control of the situation) and ordered the passengers in his boat onto the others in the bunch. Then, leaving skeleton crews on the others, he ordered all other sailors onto Boat 14 and moved back towards the spot where the *Titanic* had gone down.

But he had left it too long. He had not allowed for the rapid debilitation, unconsciousness and death caused by the plummeting temperatures. Only four people were pulled alive out of the water. But he had at least tried and his failure was one caused by miscalculation and not timidity. There were few others who that could truly be said of on this tragic night.

For those who died in the water expired not just because of the cold but also because of the vice of fear and terror that was gripping those in the half-empty boats. There was the very real fear of suction first of all. This was a genuine anxiety, given for example what the *Olympic* had done to the *Hawke* as a relatively recent reminder. It was ironic that when the *Titanic* went down there was very little suction at all, but it was very understandable that those in the boats were worried that there would be.

But worse was what happened next. The cries that went up from those suddenly fighting for their breath in the water were remarked on by so many of the survivors that the cliché that they would remember this for the rest of their lives was for once surely true. In the future, strange things would set off memories for those who were there. Young Frank Goldsmith, a boy who lost his father in the sinking, would later live near a baseball stadium and the sounds of the crowd as they cheered a home run would always take him back to the North Atlantic and those terrified screams for help.

It was the fear that this inspired – the terror that if the boats were to go back into the crowd of souls in the water they would be swamped and those in them would just be added to the list of casualties – that made those in the boats, some less than half full, hang back. Much was made after the disaster of the heroism – and heroism there was, alongside sacrifice and a real concern for others. But there were all those other human emotions too: fear, a selfish though normal desire to survive, that driving force of self-preservation. And it was this last less heroic but very commonplace human emotion which explains finally why 500 people in the water, who did not need to die, perished along with 1,000 others for whom mathematically there was no hope.

The cries died down and then stopped altogether. Those who had lived amongst so much death were left alone with their fears, their terrors and their haunted memories. As the disconsolate survivors in the boats kept their weary vigil, hoping against hope that a rescue ship might be sighted soon, it became apparent that even in the smaller details the White Star Line had let them down. The boats were supposed to be provisioned with reserves of food and water just in case. Few looked for them but it is not at all clear that all the boats had these provisions. But more important in the darkness was the fact that the boats should also have had lights. Yet these had not been handed out to all of them and this made it clearly more difficult to know where other boats were and coordinate their efforts to stay together.

It probably did not make much difference as it happened, but it might have done. It was another piece of sloppiness and lack of detailed planning that epitomised the carelessness of the shipping line. Underlying it all of course was an attitude. This was one of complacency, of failing to allow for the worst-case scenario. For no one believed that it would be necessary to worry very much about safety on the *Titanic*. Her design, her watertight compartments, her sheer vastness – all combined to make her impervious to anything nature could throw at her.

It was an attitude that would die with the ship and the hundreds of wasted lives that were cut short in this all too avoidable disaster. It was this attitude that led to the loss of the ship and had then compounded this already grave tragedy by condemning 1,500 people to death when there were two hours and forty minutes to fill lifeboats that could easily have been provided for everyone and lowered with no problems at all onto a flat calm sea. In terms of maritime safety, nothing would be the same again after the morning of 15 April 1912.

The upturned collapsible threatened to sink as dawn broke and Lightoller, taking control of a situation as an officer could, summoned another boat across to help. He had already performed stoically during the night, getting those perched precariously atop the upturned boat to move to one side or the other as the swell picked up to stop it from turning over. All those still alive on the collapsible were transferred over, resulting in about seventy-five people being aboard.

But now at last there was hope, a ship coming slowly towards them, dodging the ice. She was no superliner, her passengers were not of the 'smart set', this was no 'millionaire's special'. She moved slowly, cautiously, without much in the way of elegance or style. But she represented safety, security, survival. Meanwhile 2 miles down in the North Atlantic a floating palace, floating no more, began a long, slow process of decline and decay just moments into her short and tragic life. For those who were there, and indeed for all who would sail the seas after her, a new world had begun.

For a time, no one could quite believe what had happened. The White Star Line issued a press release in New York, saying that 'the *Titanic* was the last word in shipbuilding. Every regulation prescribed by the British Board of Trade has been complied with. The master, officers, and crew were the most experienced and skilled in the British service.' It was as if she was still believed unsinkable. And yet, she had sunk.

Those who survived returned to their lives, changed for ever. For some it was as if life had started anew. Second-class passenger Lawrence Beesley resolved to hang on to every moment of life as if each one was precious. But for many it was a life of mourning, of shattered dreams, of attempts to put those awful moments out of their minds, locked up in a cupboard. But they refused to stay locked away and would continually haunt the waking and sleeping moments of those who had borne the unbearable and now struggled to survive.

9

THE LESSONS OF THE *TITANIC*

It was clear that the loss of this great ship could have been avoided if at any stage an action had been taken to intervene with the chain reaction. If the ice warnings had been taken seriously and plotted more meticulously on the charts – and then the officers had taken the trouble to look at them – then things might have turned out rather differently. If they had diverted their course or slowed down then they almost certainly would have done.

Posting more lookouts – and giving them some of the binoculars that were freely available to the officers of the bridge – might also have helped though this is far less certain given the strange atmospherics around that night. There was no substitute really for the inconvenient but certainly far safer options of reducing speed or moving out of the way of the ice.

There was little doubt too that extending the bulkheads up and installing the double bottom up the sides would also have made the ship safer. Then of course the provision of lifeboats for all would have made a difference, as would making sure that everybody on board knew where their boat was in times of trouble. Lifeboat drill was clearly crucial too. And it was obviously sensible that wireless operators should be operating, in twenty-first-century parlance, 24/7 – as was also using rockets only as distress signals rather than 'hello, how are you?' messages in the middle of the night.

Much of this was immediately apparent at the time. Ships such as the *Olympic* ensured that there were 'boats for all' long before any new laws were passed (Bruce Ismay was making sure of that even as he stepped off the *Carpathia* in New York). The Ice Patrol would soon be doing its utmost to ensure that ships were informed and moved out of the way in plenty of time to avoid trouble. Boat drills, as anyone who frequents modern cruise liners will know, are now standard practice, wireless operators no longer leave their apparatus unattended, and safety has a far higher priority than ever.

Much of this can be traced back to the *Titanic* disaster. Of course, many changes may well have occurred over time anyway. But there can be no doubt that this particular catastrophe acted as a catalyst, a clarion call to the world to wake up that could not be ignored. Despite the futile waste of millions of lives in world wars and other conflicts ever since, the story itself lives on, perhaps the most poignant of all shipping disasters even now.

These changes of course made shipping much safer and for that anyone who steps on a ship now should breathe a little prayer of thanks for the impact of this timeless tragedy. And yet ...

Just two years later, the *Storstad* slammed into the side of the *Empress of Ireland*. The collier had been seen by the passenger liner some time before the former disappeared into a fog. When the collier was next seen, it was as she materialised from out of the deadly mist and slammed headlong into the side of the liner (that is one version; another is that the *Empress* cut across the bow of the *Storstad*). The *Empress of Ireland* had watertight compartments but she sank in fourteen minutes. Her wireless operator had time to send out an SOS but no one could respond to it in time. There were forty lifeboats on board but there was only time to launch four of them. One way or the other, human error was responsible for the loss of 1,012 lives (more passengers were actually lost on the *Empress* than the *Titanic*, though the latter had much higher numbers of dead amongst the crew).

The year after came the *Lusitania* disaster. She went down in eighteen minutes after being hit by a torpedo despite the fact that her watertight compartments made her much more robust than the *Titanic*. The steep angle of the deck as she listed meant that of her forty-eight lifeboats only six could be launched. Then in 1916 it was the turn of the *Britannic*. She had of course been fitted out with extra safety features that supposedly made her far more robust than the *Titanic*. Yet she sank in less than an hour.

Safety improvements made possible by modern technology should of course make things less hazardous. Yet that imponderable known as 'attitude' still plays havoc. It certainly did so in the case of the *Herald of Free Enterprise*. And it did too with the *Dona Paz*. She was a ferry plying her trade in the Philippines when she collided with an oil tanker in 1987. What followed made the *Titanic* look a masterpiece of damage limitation by comparison.

There were no lifebelts for passengers and no crew giving orders to passengers. The lights soon failed. A fire broke out on the oil tanker and spread to the *Dona Paz*. There was no radio to send out any desperate pleas for help. Only twenty-four people were picked up alive out of the water. The first official death toll was one of 1,749 people, worse even than the *Titanic*. But that was not the end of it. Stories grew that there were hundreds, thousands even, of passengers who were not on the manifest. Within a few days of the sinking, twenty-one bodies had been formally identified; only one of them was officially on the passenger list. Most estimates of the death toll now put it at over 4,000, a quite horrifying figure.

Was this human error or was it something worse? This was no honest mistake; this was recklessness on a cataclysmic scale. It implies something far beyond mere carelessness – that life is cheap and not in most cases worth very much. So too it was for at least some of those on the *Titanic*, a story of tragedy and pathos and yet a disaster that was also altogether avoidable. Perhaps not enough has changed since that fateful night of 14/15 April 1912.

SELECT BIBLIOGRAPHY

This is by no means a comprehensive list, which would be hundreds of items long given its extent, but rather a pointer for those who wish to explore the mysteries of the *Titanic* further. The most important sources though are primary, particularly the transcripts of the two major post-disaster enquiries. These are freely available in a number of places but the source used here is the Paperless Archives of the Titanic Historical Document Archive (www.paperlessarchives.com).

In addition, a number of survivors wrote personal accounts after the sinking. Although these are available individually, many of them have been brought together in *The Story of the Titanic as Told by its Survivors* (edited by Jack Winocour, Dover Publications, Mineola, New York, 1960). Included here are the stories of Gracie, Beesley, Bride and Lightoller. Gracie's account is also included in *Titanic: A Survivor's Story* (Chicago, 1998) which also includes the account of the (at the time) young Jack Thayer. For the crews' perspective, a fascinating insight is given in *Titanic Voices: Memories from the Fateful Voyage* (written, compiled and edited by Donald Hyslop, Alastair Forsyth and Sheila Jemima, Sutton Publishing, Stroud, 1997). Violet Jessop's story is told with verve in *Titanic Survivor: The Memoirs of Violet Jessop, Stewardess* (edited by John Maxtone-Graham, Sutton Publishing, 1998, reprinted 2007).

The classic version of the sinking as a whole remains Walter Lord's *A Night to Remember*, first published in 1956, republished many times since. In addition, Lord wrote a 'sequel' looking at various aspects in particular, published as *The Night Lives On*, (Harmondsworth, 1978). A comprehensive account is also found in Eaton and Haas, *Titanic: Triumph and Tragedy – A Chronicle in Words and Pictures* (Patrick Stephens Limited, Yeovil, Somerset, 1995 edition). Readers can also refer to my own *Titanic: Nine Hours to Hell* (Amberley Publishing, Stroud, 2010, reprinted 2011). *The Complete Titanic* by Stephen J. Spignesi (Birch Lane Press, Secaucus, New Jersey, 1998) is something of a miscellany but does bring some interesting materials together.

Two personal favourites are *The Titanic: End of a Dream* (Wyn Craig Wade, Weidenfeld & Nicholson, London, 1980 edition), which looks at the conduct of the American enquiry, and Professor Stephanie Barczewski's *Titanic: A Night Remembered* (Hambledon Continuum, London and New York, 2006), superbly written by a professional historian and full of insights into the impact of the disaster on the various communities affected in the United Kingdom. The recent *Titanic* by Anton Gill which accompanied a Channel 4 series (4 Books, 2010) looks at the construction of the ship.

Two other recent offerings which look at different aspects of the sinking and shed some chinks of light on them include Frances Wilson's *How to Survive the Titanic, or the Sinking of J. Bruce Ismay* (Bloomsbury, London, 2011) and *Racing Through the Night: Olympic's Attempt to Reach Titanic* by Wade Sisson (Amberley Publishing, 2011).

The subplot around the *Californian* has a genre all of its own. Those siding with Captain Lord include Peter Padfield in *The Titanic and the Californian* (Hodder & Stoughton, London, 1965), Senan Molony in *The Titanic and the Mystery Ship* (Tempus, Stroud, 2006) and Thomas B. Williams in *Titanic and the Californian* (edited and revised by Rob Kamps, Tempus, 2007). In the opposite corner sit Leslie Reade in *The Ship That Stood Still* (edited and updated by Edward P. de Groot, Patrick Stephens Limited, Yeovil, 1993) and Daniel Allen Butler in *The Other Side of the Night* (Casemate, Philadelphia and Newbury, 2009). A problem with the whole sorry tale is that authors can pick and choose the bits of contradictory evidence that suit their own particular case and ignore the others.

Finally, there is a mass of information available on the internet. There are some particularly outstanding websites, of which a personal favourite is the Encyclopedia Titanica (www.encyclopedia-titanica.org). For those who wish to stay in touch with all things *Titanic*, the Titanic Historic Society is also of interest (http://www. titanic1.org).

LIST OF ILLUSTRATIONS

Also available from Amberley Publishing

The story of the sinking of the Titanic *based on first-hand accounts collected in the days and weeks following the disaster*

'If you only read one book about *Titanic*, read this one; if you've read every book published about the *Titanic*, read this one again' NAUTILUS INTENATIONAL TELEGRAPH

On Thursday 22 May 1912, a mere 37 days after the sinking, respected London publisher Grant Richards, delivered Filson Young's book to booksellers around the capital. Both Filson and Grant knew victims of the sinking and both worked hard to gather first-hand testimony to use in the book. Much of his telling of the story still stands today and his speculations about the feeling of daily life aboard the doomed ship are used in books and films on the subject.

£16.99 Hardback
92 illustrations
160 pages
978-1-4456-0407-7

Available from all good bookshops or to order direct
Please call **01453-847-800**
www.amberleybooks.com

Also Available from Amberley Publishing

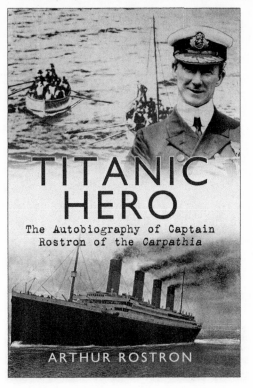

The story of the Titanic in the words of the hero who's swift action saved the lives of over 700 survivors

'A gem... Arthur Rostron was actually there, and his account is about real people and the practicalities of helping them'
NAUTILUS INTERNATIONAL TELEGRAPH

£16.99 Paperback
39 illustrations
192 pages
978-1-4456-0420-6

Available from all good bookshops or to order direct
Please call **01453-847-800**
www.amberleybooks.com

Available from December 2011 from Amberley Publishing

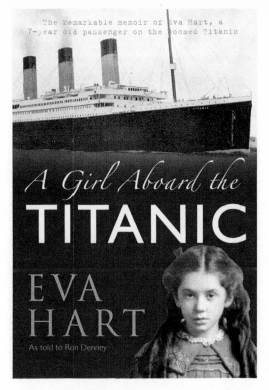

The remarkable memoir of Eva Hart, a 7-year old passenger on the doomed Titanic

'I saw that ship sink, I never closed my eyes. I saw it, I heard it, and nobody could possibly forget it. I can remember the colours, the sounds, everything. The worst thing I can remember are the screams'. This is the amazing story of how Eva survived the sinking of the *Titanic* and the affect it had on her life following the tragedy. The events of a few hours in her childhood remained with her so vividly throughout her life that it took Eva nearly forty years before she could talk openly about the tragedy.

£16.99 Hardback
60 illustrations
192 pages
978-1-4456-0089-5

Available from December 2011 from all good bookshops or to order direct
Please call **01453-847-800**
www.amberleybooks.com

Also available from Amberley Publishing

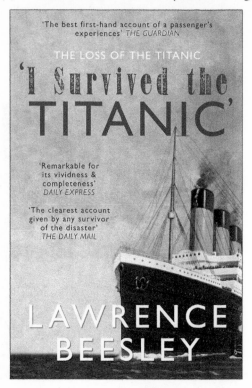

The first-hand account of the sinking of the Titanic by second class
passenger and Englishman, Lawrence Beesley, the longest and most
detailed memoir of the sinking

'The best first-hand account of a passenger's experiences... a first-rate piece of descriptive writing'
THE GUARDIAN
'Remarkable for its vividness and completeness' THE DAILY EXPRESS
'The clearest account given by any survivor of the disaster' THE DAILY MAIL
'Thrilling' THE SPECTATOR
'As authoritative and comprehensive an account of the greatest marine disaster of modern times as will ever be
written' NEW YORK TIMES

£16.99 Hardback
68 illustrations
192 pages
978-1-4456-0443-5

Available from all good bookshops or to order direct
Please call **01453-847-800**
www.amberleybooks.com

Also available from Amberley Publishing

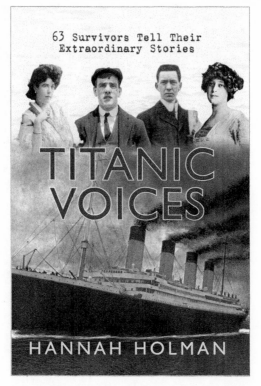

The sinking of the Titanic *in the words of the survivors*

There were 712 survivors of the *Titanic* disaster and their horrific experience has captivated readers and movie goers for almost 100 years. But what was it actually like for a woman to say goodbye to her husband? For a mother to leave her teenage sons? For the unlucky many who found themselves in the freezing Atlantic waters? *Titanic Voices* is the most comprehensive collection of *Titanic* survivors' accounts ever published and includes many unpublished, and long forgotten accounts, unabridged, together with an authoritative editorial commentary. It is also the first book to include substantial accounts from women survivors - most of the previously well known accounts were written by men.

£20 Hardback
135 illustrations (11 colour)
512 pages
978-1-4456-0222-6

Available from all good bookshops or to order direct
Please call **01453-847-800**
www.amberleybooks.com

Also available from Amberley Publishing

A major new history of the disaster that weaves into the narrative the first-hand accounts of those who survived

· 'Enthralling' THE DAILY MAIL
'Quite the best and most level-headed telling of the whole story I have ever read'
THE INDEPENDENT ON SUNDAY

It was twenty minutes to midnight on Sunday 14 April, when Jack Thayer felt the Titanic lurch to port, a motion followed by the slightest of shocks. Seven-year old Eva Hart barely noticed anything was wrong. For Stoker Fred Barrett, shovelling coal down below, it was somewhat different; the side of the ship where he was working caved in. For the next nine hours, Jack, Eva and Fred faced death and survived. 1600 people did not. This is the story told through the eyes of Jack, Eva, Fred and over a hundred others of those who survived and recorded their experiences.

£9.99 Paperback
72 illustrations (14 colour)
368 pages
978-1-4456-0482-4

Available from all good bookshops or to order direct
Please call **01453-847-800**
www.amberleybooks.com

INDEX